**BEHAVIOR** A sea otter can stay underwater for up to four minutes.

**HABITAT** Sea otters live in the Pacific Ocean along the coast of California.

D0603611

**YOUNG** A sea otter pup can not swim when it is born. It rests on its mother's stomach.

**BEHAVIOR** Sea otters wrap kelp around their bodies when they sleep.

# California
# Science

**Harcourt**
SCHOOL PUBLISHERS

Visit *The Learning Site!*
www.harcourtschool.com

# California
# Science

Sea otters

## Series Consulting Authors

**Michael J. Bell, Ph.D.**
Assistant Professor of Early
  Childhood Education
College of Education
West Chester University of
  Pennsylvania
West Chester, Pennsylvania

**Michael A. DiSpezio**
Curriculum Architect
JASON Academy
Cape Cod, Massachusetts

**Marjorie Frank**
Former Adjunct, Science
  Education
Hunter College
New York, New York

**Gerald H. Krockover, Ph.D.**
Professor of Earth and
  Atmospheric Science
  Education
Purdue University
West Lafayette, Indiana

**Joyce C. McLeod**
Adjunct Professor
Rollins College
Winter Park, Florida

**Barbara ten Brink, Ph.D.**
Science Specialist
Austin Independent School
  District
Austin, Texas

**Carol J. Valenta**
Senior Vice President
St. Louis Science Center
St. Louis, Missouri
Former teacher, principal,
  and Coordinator of
  Science Center
  Instructional Programs
Los Angeles Unified School
  District
Los Angeles, California

**Barry A. Van Deman**
President and CEO
Museum of Life and Science
Durham, North Carolina

SCHOOL PUBLISHERS

Science and Technology features
provided by

## Introductory Unit
# Ready, Set, Science!

**Big Idea** Scientists find out about things by asking questions and doing investigations.

**Essential Questions**

# PHYSICAL SCIENCE

Temecula Valley
Balloon Festival

# LIFE SCIENCE

## UNIT 2 Plants and Animals Meet Their Needs 130

**Big Idea** Plants and animals need some things to live and grow. They meet their needs in different ways.

# EARTH SCIENCE

## Unit 3 Weather

**Big Idea** People can observe, measure, and describe weather.

## References

# Ready, Set, Science!

**4** Scientific progress is made by asking meaningful questions and conducting careful investigations. As a basis for understanding this concept and addressing the content in the other three strands, students should develop their own questions and perform investigations. Students will:

**4.a** Draw pictures that portray some features of the thing being described.

**4.b** Record observations and data with pictures, numbers, or written statements.

**4.c** Record observations on a bar graph.

**4.d** Describe the relative position of objects by using two references (e.g., above and next to, below and left of).

**4.e** Make new observations when discrepancies exist between two descriptions of the same object or phenomenon.

## What's the Big Idea?

Scientists find out about things by asking questions and doing investigations.

## Essential Questions

KidZone
Youth Museum
Hemet, California

Dear Malcolm,

At KidZone, I observed how water moves into our homes. I even dug for dinosaur bones, like a real scientist. I wish you could have been there!

John

Read John's postcard. What did John learn about being a scientist? How do you think that helps explain the **Big Idea?**

1

## Investigation and Experimentation

**4.b** Record observations and data with pictures, numbers, or written statements.

### LESSON 1

**Essential Question**

# How Do We Use Investigation Skills?

## California Fast Fact

### California Oranges

You can compare oranges by the way they taste. Oranges on high branches are usually sweeter than those on low branches. What are some other ways you can compare oranges?

2

**investigation skills**

p. 6

**observe** p. 10

California oranges

# Fruit Protection

## Ask a Question

Observe and compare the peels of these fruits. How are they alike? How are they different?

kiwi

pineapple

## Get Ready

**Investigation Skill Tip**
When you observe, you use your senses to find out about things. You can use pictures, numbers, or words to record what you see.

### You need

fruits

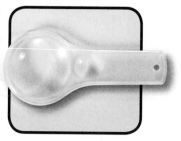

hand lens

4

## What to Do

**Step ①**

Observe some fruits with a hand lens. Look at their peels.

**Step ②**

Observe the cut fruits with the hand lens. What is inside the fruits?

**Step ③**

Draw a picture to record what you see.

## Draw Conclusions

How do peels protect the insides of fruits?

### Independent Inquiry

Find pictures of plants that have thorns or bark. **Draw a conclusion** about why plants have these kinds of coverings.

4.b

**VOCABULARY**
investigation skills
observe

**Focus Skill** **MAIN IDEA AND DETAILS**

Look for details about the
investigation skills scientists use.

# Using Investigation Skills

Scientists use investigation skills
when they do tests. **Investigation
skills** help people find out about things.
You can use these skills, too.

communicate, or tell

classify

hypothesize

draw conclusions

sequence

egg

larva

pupa

butterfly comes out

adult butterfly

make a model

Sun

Earth

compare

measure

9

When you **observe**, you use your senses to find out about things.

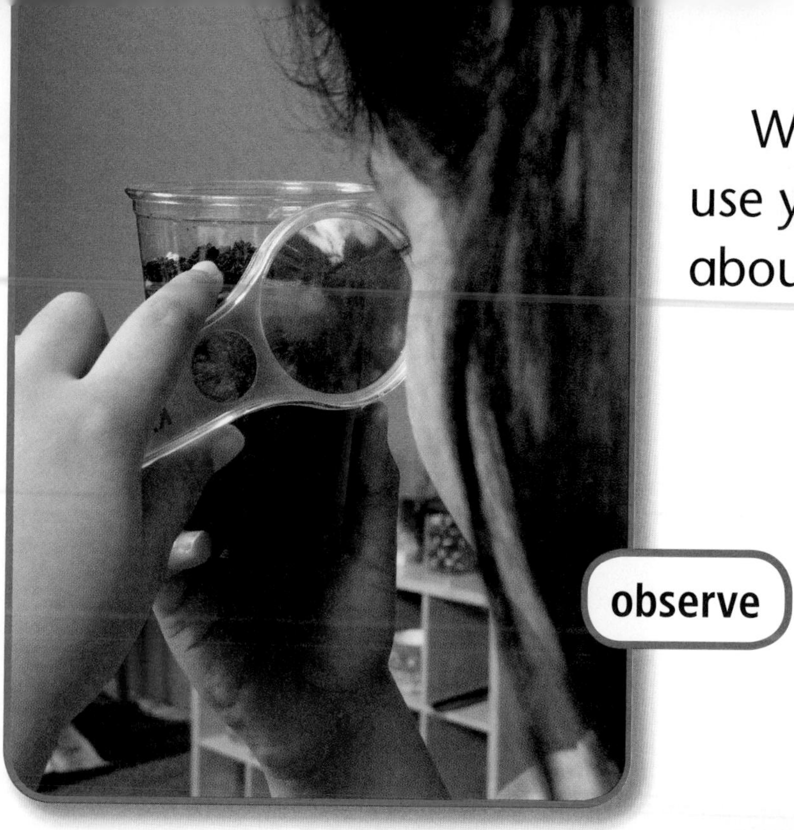
observe

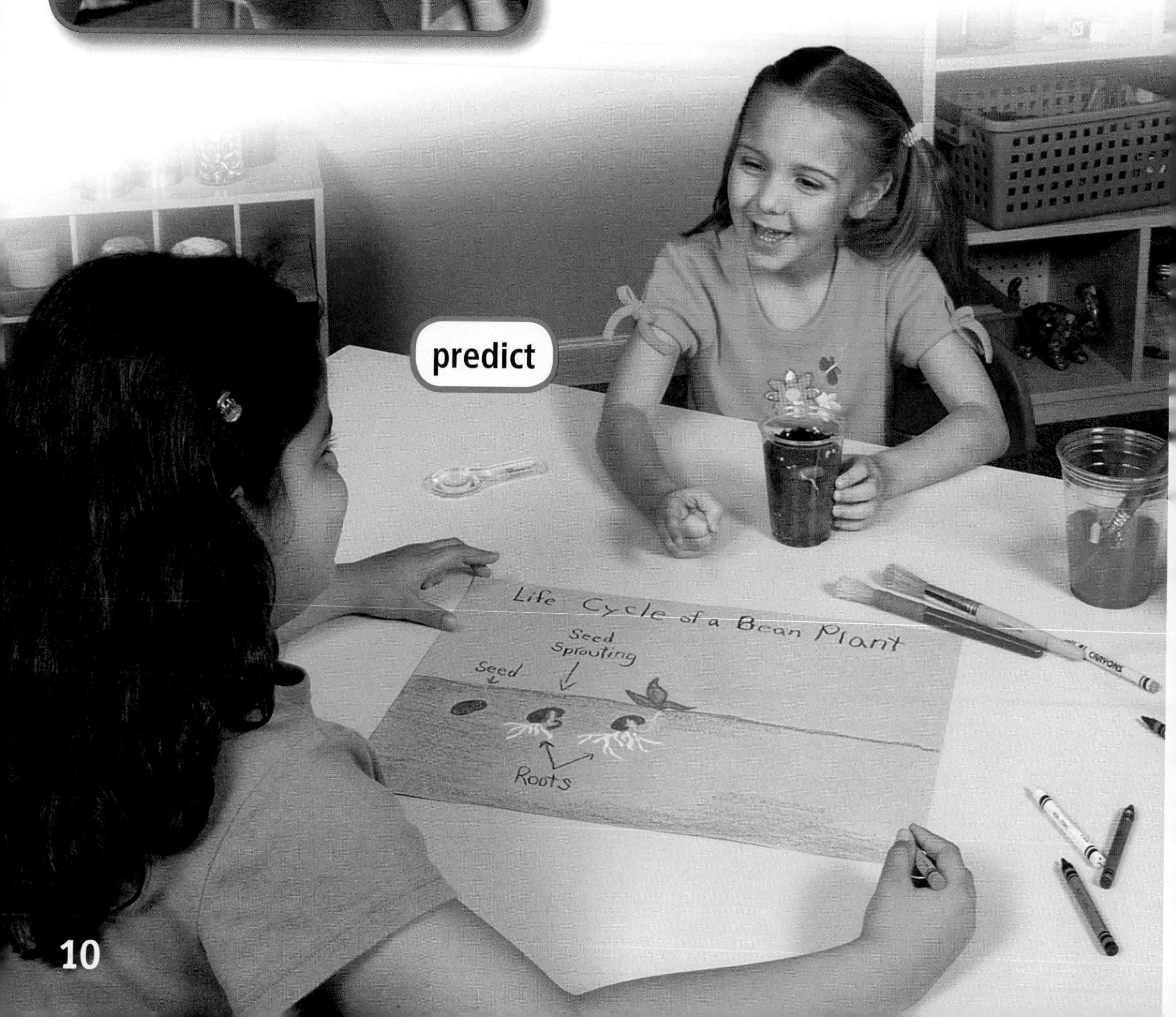
predict
Life Cycle of a Bean Plant
Seed Sprouting
Seed
Roots
CRAYONS

plan an investigation

infer

Focus Skill **MAIN IDEA AND DETAILS**

What skills do scientists use when they do tests?

## Insta-Lab

### How Far Will It Roll?

Get a ball. Predict how far it will go if you roll it across the floor. Mark that spot with tape. Then roll the ball. Was your prediction correct?

## Essential Question

**How do we use investigation skills?**

In this lesson, you learned about investigation skills that help scientists observe, find out about things, and test ideas.

**Investigation and Experimentation Standards in This Lesson**

**4.b** Record observations and data with pictures, numbers, or written statements.

1. **MAIN IDEA AND DETAILS** Make a chart like this one. Show details for this main idea. **Investigation skills help people find out about things**. **4.b**

```
        Main Idea
       /    |    \
  detail  detail  detail
```

2. **DRAW CONCLUSIONS** How can a model help you find out about something? **4.b**

3. **VOCABULARY** Use the words **investigation skills** to tell about this picture. **4.b**

4. **Critical Thinking** What should you do to find out how long a pencil is? **4.b**

5. What do you do when you observe? **4.b**
   A group things
   B make a guess
   C make a plan
   D use your senses

## The Big Idea

6. How do investigation skills help you observe, find out about things, and test ideas? **4.b**

## Writing ELA– WS 2.2

### Write to Describe

1. Use clay to make a model of your favorite animal.

2. List words that describe your animal.

3. Share your model and your list with the class.

My Dog
furry
Soft
black

## Math SDAP I.I

### Grouping Blocks

1. Get some blocks that are different sizes and colors.

2. Classify the blocks by both size and color.

3. Draw a picture that shows how you classified the blocks.

For more links and activities, go to **www.hspscience.com**

## Investigation and Experimentation

**4.b** Record observations and data with pictures, numbers, or written statements.

**LESSON 2**

Essential Question

# How Do We Use Science Tools?

## California Fast Fact

### Weighing Fruit

People can buy fruit at markets. They can weigh the fruit on a scale. A scale is a tool used to find out how heavy an object is.

14

## Vocabulary Preview

**science tools** p. 18

weighing fruit at a
California market

15

# Compare Fruit

## Ask a Question

What tool are these people using?

## Get Ready

**Investigation Skill Tip**
When you compare objects, you see how they are alike and different. You can draw pictures to show how you compare objects.

### You need

strawberry

pear

balance

## What to Do

**Step ①**

Put one piece of fruit on each side of a balance.

**Step ②**

**Compare** the masses of the fruits.

**Step ③**

Draw a picture to record what you see.

## Draw Conclusions

Which fruit has less mass? Which fruit has more mass?

**Independent Inquiry**

Measure around two fruits. **Compare** the measurements. Which fruit is bigger around? 4.b

## Using Science Tools

Scientists use tools to find out about things. You can use tools to find out about things, too. **Science tools** help people do investigations. They help you observe, compare, and measure things.

Some things have parts that are too small to see. You can use a hand lens or a magnifying box to help you see them.

hand lens and magnifying box

18

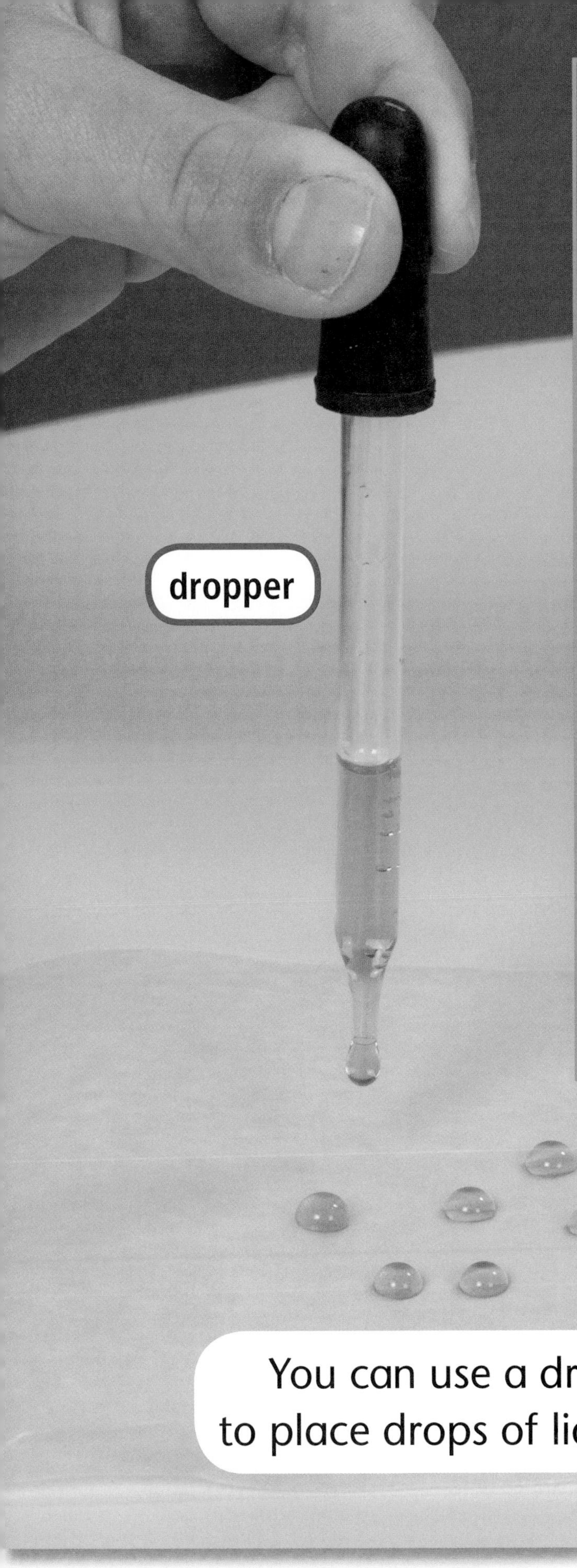

dropper

forceps

You can use forceps
to help you hold or
separate things.

You can use a dropper
to place drops of liquid.

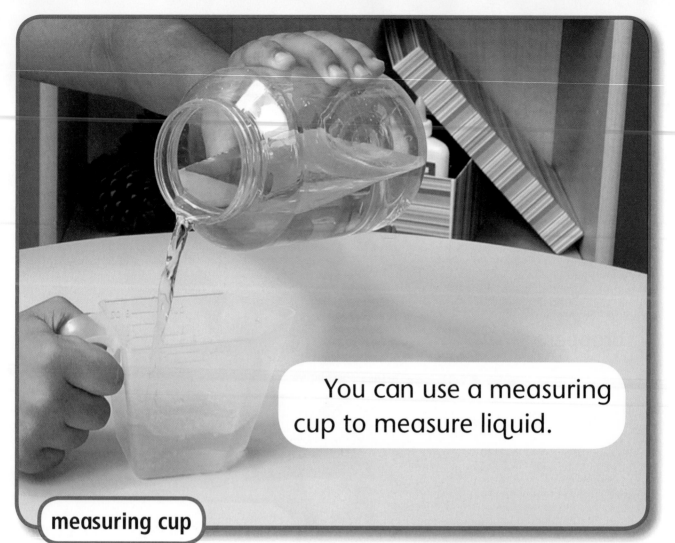

You can use a measuring cup to measure liquid.

**measuring cup**

You can use a thermometer to measure how warm or cold something is.

**thermometer**

You can use a ruler to measure how long or tall an object is. You can use a tape measure to measure around an object.

You can use a balance to measure the mass of an object.

Focus Skill **MAIN IDEA AND DETAILS** How can you use science tools to find out information?

**Measure It!**
Use a tape measure to measure around one arm. Then measure around a leg. Compare the numbers. Which one is greater?

balance

ruler

tape measure

21

Essential Question

**Investigation and Experimentation Standards in This Lesson**

**How do we use science tools?**

In this lesson, you learned how to use science tools to observe, compare, and measure things.

**4.b** Record observations and data with pictures, numbers, or written statements.

**1.** (Focus Skill) MAIN IDEA AND DETAILS

Make a chart like this one. Show details of this main idea. **You can use science tools**. **4.b**

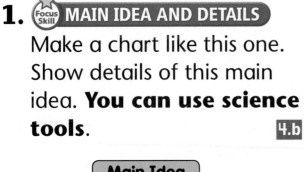

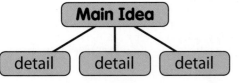

**2. SUMMARIZE** Tell ways to use science tools to find out about things. **4.b**

**3. VOCABULARY** Use the words **science tools** to tell about the picture. **4.b**

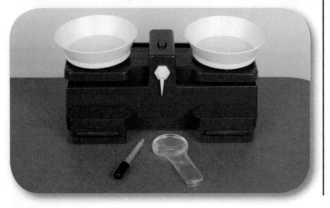

**4. Critical Thinking** Look at these science tools. Which one would you use to make something look larger? **4.b**

**5.** How are a ruler and tape measure alike? How are they different? **4.b**

## The **Big Idea**

**6.** How do science tools help you observe, compare, and measure things? **4.b**

### Writing  ELA–WS 2.2

## Write to Describe

1. Name a science tool you have used.

2. Draw a picture of the tool.

3. Write one sentence about how you used the tool.

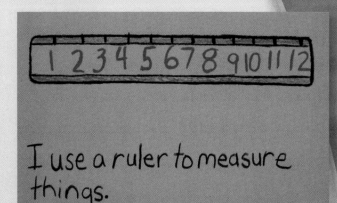

I use a ruler to measure things.

### Math  NS 1.2

## Estimate and Count

1. Estimate how many cotton balls it will take to fill a measuring cup. Then fill the cup with cotton balls.

2. How many cotton balls did you need? Use > or < to tell if the number of cotton balls was greater or less than the number you estimated.

For more links and activities, go to **www.hspscience.com**

## Investigation and Experimentation

**4.a** Draw pictures that portray some features of the thing being described.

**4.d** Describe the relative position of objects by using two references (e.g., above and next to, below and left of).

**4.e** Make new observations when discrepancies exist between two descriptions of the same object or phenomenon.

**Essential Question**

# How Can We Describe the Position of Objects?

## California Fast Fact

### Growing Fruits

The peach is California's state fruit. Peaches are grown in the San Joaquin Valley. San Joaquin is next to Sacramento.

**San Joaquin Valley**

**above** p. 30

**below** p. 31

25

# Position of Objects

## Ask a Question

Look at this picture. How would you tell where the book is?

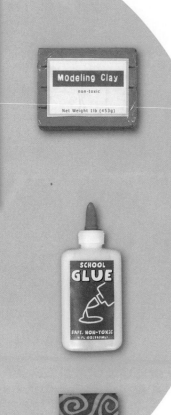

## Get Ready

**Investigation Skill Tip**
You **tell** something to a person to communicate, or share information, with that person.

**You need**

fruits

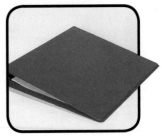

folder

# What to Do

**Step ①**

Place your fruits behind the folder.

**Step ②**

**Tell** your partner how to make his or her fruits match yours. Use words like **above** and **next to**.

**Step ③**

Remove the folder. Compare where the fruits are. If they look different, then repeat the Investigate.

## Draw Conclusions

What did you learn about describing where things are?  4.d

**Independent Inquiry**

**Tell** a partner to draw a picture by using your directions. Use words like **above** and **below**.  4.a, 4.d

27

**VOCABULARY**
above
below

⭐ **MAIN IDEA AND DETAILS**

Look for the main ideas about how to tell where things are.

# Positions of Objects

You can use words to tell where things are.

⭐ **MAIN IDEA AND DETAILS** What are two words you can use to tell where the helicopter is?

left

next to

out

below

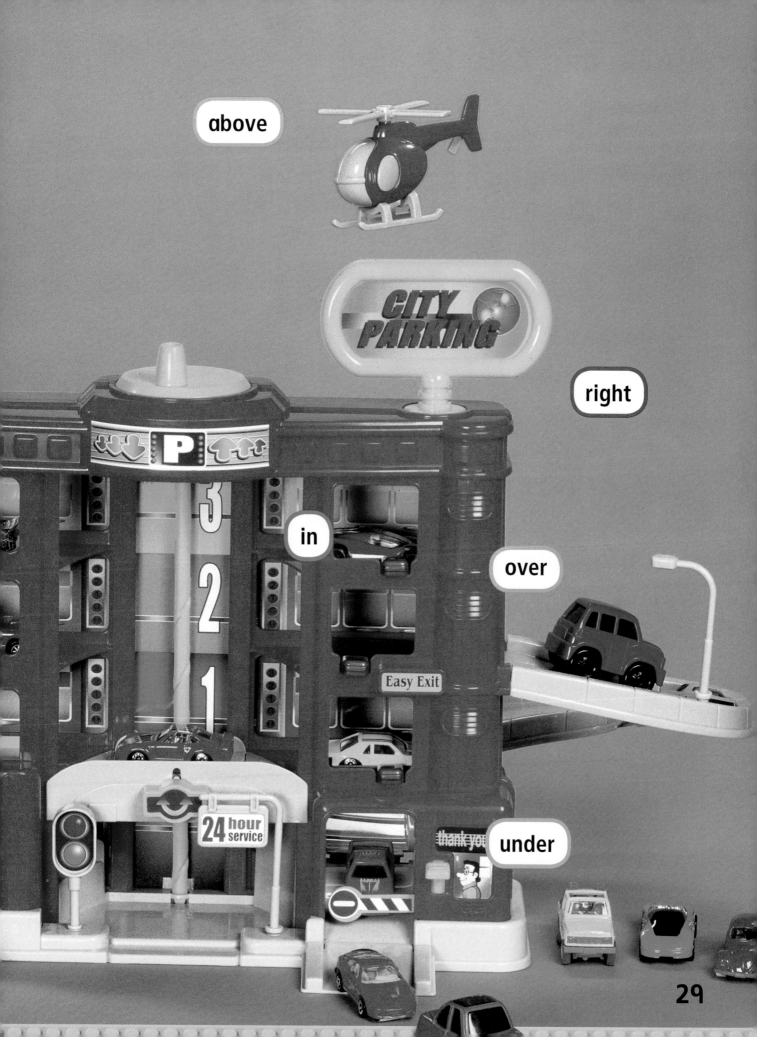

above

right

in

over

under

# Above and Below

Above and below are words you can use to tell where things are. **Above** means that a thing is at a higher place. The firefighter is above the truck.

above

**Below** means that a thing is at a lower place. The orange car is below the blue car.

⭐ **MAIN IDEA AND DETAILS**

**What other things are below the blue car?**

**Insta-Lab**

**Secret Art**

Make a piece of art behind a folder. Place it in the classroom with other pieces. Describe your art to the class by using words like **above** and **below**. See if your classmates can guess which art is yours.

below

31

## Essential Question

**How can we describe the position of objects?**

In this lesson, you learned that you can use words to tell where things are.

**Investigation and Experimentation Standards in This Lesson**

**4.d** Describe the relative position of objects by using two references (e.g., above and next to, below and left of).

**1.** **Focus Skill** **MAIN IDEA AND DETAILS**

Make a chart like this one. Show details of this main idea. **You can use words to tell where things are.** **4.d**

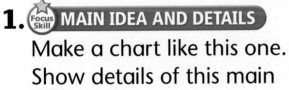

**2.** **SUMMARIZE** Tell what you have learned about how to tell where things are. **4.d**

**3.** **VOCABULARY** Use the words **above** and **below** to tell about this picture. **4.d**

**4. Investigation** When should you repeat an Investigate? **4.e**

**5.** What are two words you can use to tell where the driver is? **4.d**

## The **Big Idea**

**6.** Draw a picture. Label the things in your picture. Tell where each thing is. **4.d**

### Writing ELA–WS 2.2

## Write to Describe

1. Look up. What is above you? Now look down. What is below you?

2. Draw a picture with you in the middle of it.

3. Draw the things you see above and below you. Label each thing.

### Math MG 1.0, 1.1

## Measure Positions

1. Put an eraser in the center of your desk.

2. Measure 3 paper clips above the eraser. Put a pencil there. Measure 5 paper clips below the eraser. Put a marker there.

3. Describe the positions of the pencil and marker.

For more links and activities, go to **www.hspscience.com**

## Investigation and Experimentation

**4.b** Record observations and data with pictures, numbers, or written statements.

**4.c** Record observations on a bar graph.

**4.e** Make new observations when discrepancies exist between two descriptions of the same object or phenomenon.

Essential Question

# How Do Scientists Work?

## California Fast Fact

### Half Moon Bay Art and Pumpkin Festival

Some of the pumpkins at this festival weigh more than 454 kilograms (1000 pounds). That is as much as a full-grown cow! Why do you think this pumpkin grew so big?

Number of Fruits

**bar graph** p. 43

Half Moon Bay,
California

# Measure Fruits

Directed Inquiry

## Ask a Question

Look at these things. Which one would you measure with a tape measure? Which one would you measure with a ruler?

## Get Ready

**Investigation Skill Tip**

When you plan an investigation, you think of what you need to do to find out what you want to know.

**You need**

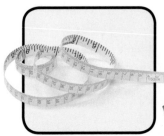 

tape measure

ruler

fruits

## What to Do

**Step 1**

How can you measure fruits? Think about it. **Plan an investigation.** Write a plan to find out.

**Step 2**

Follow your plan to investigate your ideas.

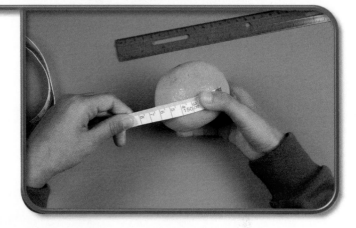

**Step 3**

Record what you observe. Share with the class what you learned.

## Draw Conclusions

What did you find out about how to measure fruits?

**Independent Inquiry**

How can you use a straw, a string, and a craft stick to move a block? **Plan an investigation** to find out.

4.b

**VOCABULARY**
bar graph

Look for the main ideas about the steps that scientists use to work.

# Investigating

Scientists follow steps to test the things they want to learn about.

**1** **Observe. Then ask a question.**

Think of a question you want to answer. What do you want to know?

Is a balloon filled with air heavier than a balloon without air?

**Form a hypothesis.**

What do you think will happen? Write an idea that you can test.

**3** **Plan a fair test.**

What do you want to learn? Write a plan. List the things you will need to do your test. List the steps you will follow.

I'll tie these at the same spot on each end.

39

**4** Do the test.

Follow the steps of your plan.
Observe. Record what happens.

**5** Draw conclusions. Tell what you learn.

What did you find out? Was your idea correct? Share your answers. Compare your answers with those of classmates. If you get different answers, do your test again.

**Focus Skill** **MAIN IDEA AND DETAILS** What steps do scientists follow to test things?

# Record What You Observe

Scientists record what they observe. You can also record what you observe. You can use pictures, words, or numbers.

You can use a bar graph to record what you observe. A **bar graph** is a way to compare things.

**Focus Skill MAIN IDEA AND DETAILS**

What are some ways you can record what you observe?

**Motion Graph**

Test some toys. Do they move in a straight path, a curved path, a zigzag path, or a circle? Record. Then make a bar graph to show how many toys move in each way.

**How do scientists work?**

In this lesson, you learned about the steps that scientists follow in order to test things.

 **Investigation and Experimentation Standards in This Lesson**

**4.b** Record observations and data with pictures, numbers, or written statements.

**4.c** Record observations on a bar graph.

**4.e** Make new observations when discrepancies exist between two descriptions of the same object or phenomenon.

**1.**  **MAIN IDEA AND DETAILS**
Make a chart like this one. Show details of this main idea. **Scientists test things they want to learn about.**    **4.b, 4.c, 4.e**

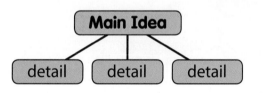

Main Idea — detail — detail — detail

**2. DRAW CONCLUSIONS**
How can you work like a scientist to test your ideas?    **4.b, 4.c, 4.e**

**3.** **VOCABULARY** Use the words **bar graph** to tell about this picture.    **4.c**

**4. Investigation** Why do scientists record what they observe?    **4.b, 4.c,**

**5.** What step follows observe and question?    **4.b**
   **A** Do the test.
   **B** Form a hypothesis.
   **C** Plan the test.
   **D** Record what you see.

The **Big Idea**

**6.** What steps do you follow when you test an idea?    **4.b, 4.c, 4.e**

### Writing   ELA–WS 2.2

## Write How to Make a Plan

1. Write a plan of what you do in the morning to get ready for school.

2. Draw three pictures to show what you do.

3. Put the pictures in order. Label them **first**, **next**, and **last**.

### Math   SDAP 1.0, 1.2

## Make a Bar Graph

1. Observe children on the playground.

2. Write how many children play on the swings, on the slide, or with a jump rope.

3. Use the data to make a bar graph.

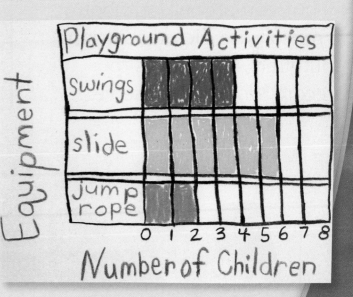

For more links and activities, go to **www.hspscience.com**

#  Wrap-Up

## ▶Visual Summary

Tell how each picture helps explain the **Big Idea**.

**The Big Idea** Scientists find out about things by asking questions and doing investigations.

**4.a, 4.b, 4.c**

You can draw pictures to show what you are talking about. You can use pictures, graphs, numbers, and words to record what you observe.

**4.d**

You can use words to tell where things are. Some of these words are **above**, **below**, **left**, and **right**.

**4.b, 4.e**

You can write a plan to find out things you want to know. Follow your plan. Record what you observe. Compare your answer with those of your classmates. If you get different answers, do your test again.

# Show What You Know

## Write to Inform

Choose a famous scientist. Go to the library. Find out about the scientist you chose. Write a paragraph about who that person is. Tell what he or she is famous for. Dress like your scientist when you read your paragraph to the class.

## Unit Project

## Think Like a Scientist

Work with a partner. Plan an investigation. Do the investigation together. Write down the steps you took to do the investigation. Write down the science tools you used. Then write down your results. Share your results with the class.

## Vocabulary Review

Use the words to complete the sentences. The page numbers tell you where to look if you need help.

**investigation skills** p. 6    **above** p. 30

**observe** p. 10                **below** p. 31

**science tools** p. 18    **bar graph** p. 43

**1.** If an object is at a higher place, it is _____.    `4.d`

**2.** Droppers and rulers are _____.    `4.b`

**3.** You can use a _____ to compare things.    `4.c`

**4.** Compare and observe are two _____.    `4.b`

**5.** When you _____, you use your senses to find out about things.    `4.b`

**6.** If an object is at a lower place, it is _____.    `4.d`

## Check Understanding

**7.** Look at these science tools. Which one would you use to measure liquid? **4.b**

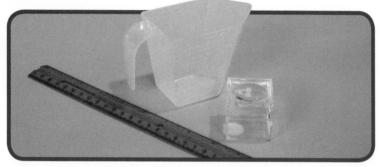

**8.** How is it helpful to draw a picture of what you are talking about? **4.a**

## Critical Thinking

**9.** You did an investigation. You and your classmates got different answers. What should you do? **4.e**

## The **Big Idea**

**10.** Tell how doing investigations, observing, and asking questions help you find out what you want to know.

# States of Matter

### California Standards in This Unit

**1** Materials come in different forms (states), including solids, liquids, and gases. As a basis for understanding this concept:

**1.a** *Students know* solids, liquids, and gases have different properties.

**1.b** *Students know* the properties of substances can change when the substances are mixed, cooled, or heated.

This unit also includes these Investigation and Experimentation Standards:

**4.a**, **4.b**, **4.c**

## What's the Big Idea?

Matter has different states. Three of these states are solid, liquid, and gas.

## Essential Questions

Los Angeles

U.S. Bank Tower

Dear Jesse,

The U.S. Bank Tower is the tallest building in California. It is made of concrete and steel. The tower is very strong. It was built to last through an earthquake!

Your friend,

Rosa

Read Rosa's postcard. What did Rosa learn about the U.S. Bank Tower? How do you think that helps explain the **Big Idea?**

## Unit Inquiry

### Solids in Water
Does a solid dissolve more easily in warm water or in cold water? Plan and do a test to find out.

![bear icon] **California Standards in This Lesson**

## Science Content

**1.a** *Students know* solids, liquids, and gases have different properties.

## Investigation and Experimentation

**4.a** Draw pictures that portray some features of the thing being described.

**4.b** Record observations and data with pictures, numbers, or written statements.

Essential Question

# What Is Matter?

## California Fast Fact

### The Golden Gate Bridge

The road on the Golden Gate Bridge is held up by cables. The wires in those cables are very long. They could wrap around Earth three times!

**matter** p. 56

**property** p. 58

**mass** p. 58

Golden Gate Bridge

# Classify Matter

**Directed Inquiry**

## Ask a Question

How can you classify these objects?

## Get Ready

**Investigation Skill Tip**
When you classify objects, you group them by how they are alike and different. You can draw pictures to show how you classify objects.

### You need

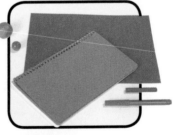

objects

## What to Do

**Step 1**

Observe the objects. Compare their sizes, shapes, and colors.

**Step 2**

**Classify** the objects in three ways.

**Step 3**

Draw pictures of the groups you made. How are the objects alike? How are they different?

## Draw Conclusions

How can you classify objects by their properties?

**1.a**

> **Independent Inquiry**
>
> Observe different rocks. **Classify** them by ways they are alike and ways they are different.
>
> **4.b**

**VOCABULARY**
matter
property
mass

⭐ **COMPARE AND CONTRAST**

Look for ways kinds of matter can be alike and different.

# Matter

Everything is **matter**. Toys are matter. Air in balloons is matter. Water is matter, too.

> **What forms of matter do you see here?**

liquid

Matter has three forms. Matter can be a solid. It can be a liquid. Matter can also be a gas.

**COMPARE AND CONTRAST**

How are the toys alike?

gas

What forms of matter do you see here?

solid

57

# Properties of Matter

You can tell what matter is like. A **property** is one part of what an object is like.

All matter has two main properties. Matter takes up space. It also has mass. **Mass** is how much matter an object has.

You can tell other things about matter. Color and shape are properties. Size is a property. Texture is a property, too. Texture is the way an object feels.

 **COMPARE AND CONTRAST**

**What are some of the properties of these objects?**

## Insta-Lab

### A Matter of Space

Choose three objects. Put them in order from the one that takes up the least space to the one that takes up the most space. Why did you order the objects the way you did?

## Essential Question

**What is matter?**

In this lesson, you learned about three kinds of matter. You also learned that different matter has different properties.

**Science Content Standards in This Lesson**

**1.a** *Students know* solids, liquids, and gases have different properties.

**1.** **Focus Skill** **COMPARE AND CONTRAST** Make a chart like this one. Use it to compare properties of matter. **1.a**

alike ——— different

**2. SUMMARIZE** Tell how kinds of matter are alike and different. **1.a**

**3. VOCABULARY** Tell about the **properties** of the block in this picture. **1.a**

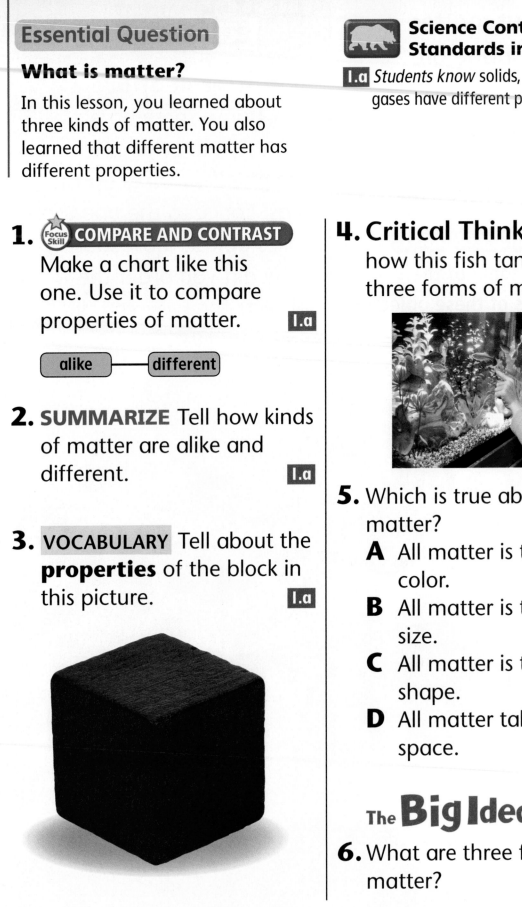

**4. Critical Thinking** Tell how this fish tank shows three forms of matter. **1.a**

**5.** Which is true about matter? **1.a**

  **A** All matter is the same color.

  **B** All matter is the same size.

  **C** All matter is the same shape.

  **D** All matter takes up space.

## The Big Idea

**6.** What are three forms of matter? **1.a**

### Writing     ELA– WS 2.2

## Write to Describe

1. Make labels for matter in your classroom.

2. On each label, name the kind of matter.

3. Then write three words that tell about it.

book
hard, heavy, purple

pencil
small, yellow, pointed

### Math     NS 1.1, SDAP 1.0, 1.1

## Graphing Matter

1. Sort the objects in your pencil box by color.

2. Count the objects in each group.

3. Make a bar graph to show your groups.

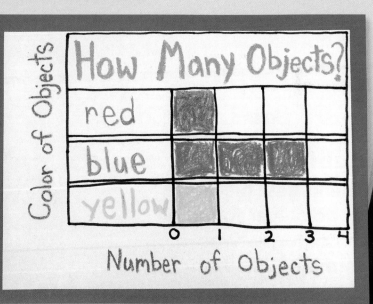

How Many Objects?

Color of Objects

red
blue
yellow

0   1   2   3   4

Number of Objects

For more links and activities, go to **www.hspscience.com**

**California Standards in This Lesson**

**Science Content**

**1.a** *Students know* solids, liquids, and gases have different properties.

**Investigation and Experimentation**

**4.b** Record observations and data with pictures, numbers, or written statements.

**Essential Question**

# What Can We Observe About Solids?

## California Fast Fact

### California Gold

The largest piece of gold ever found in California was found in Carson Hill. It weighed 88 kilograms (194 pounds). That is about what a young elephant weighs when it is born!

panning for gold

**solid** p. 67

63

# Measuring Mass

## Ask a Question

Compare the bats. Which has more mass? Compare the balls. Which has less mass?

## Get Ready

**Investigation Skill Tip**
When you compare, you look for ways things are alike and different.

**You need**

2 blocks

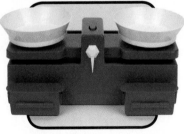

balance

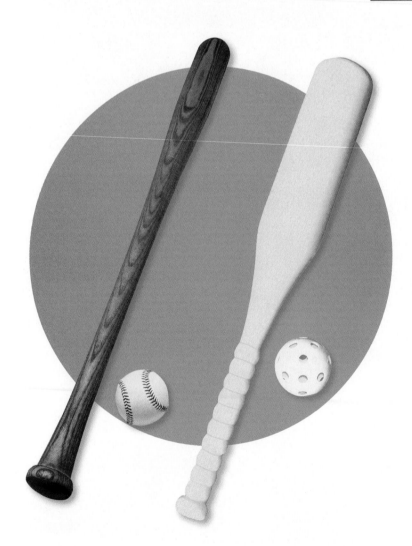

## What to Do

**Step 1**

Put a block on each side of the balance.

**Step 2**

Look at the blocks on the balance. **Compare**.

**Step 3**

Write what you observe.

## Draw Conclusions

Which block has more mass? Which has less mass?

1.a

**Independent Inquiry**

Put two solids in a bag. **Compare** the solids by using your sense of touch.

4.b

**VOCABULARY**
solid

⭐ Focus Skill **MAIN IDEA AND DETAILS**

Look for the main ideas about solids.

# Properties of Solids

How are a globe, paper, and scissors the same? They are all solids.

globe

paper

scissors

A **solid** is matter that keeps its shape even when you move it. You can see and feel a solid. It takes up space. It has mass.

(Focus Skill) **MAIN IDEA AND DETAILS** How do you know that musical instruments are solids?

musical instruments

67

# Measuring Solids

You can measure solids. You can measure how long a solid is. You measure this with a ruler.

ruler

You can measure the mass of a solid. You measure mass with a balance.

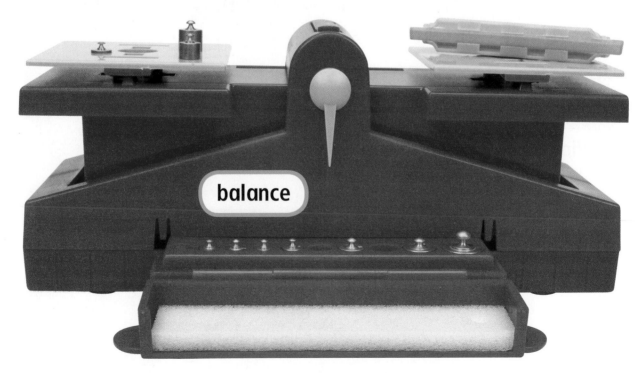

balance

You can also measure how much a solid weighs. You measure this with a scale.

**Focus Skill** MAIN IDEA AND DETAILS

What are three ways you can measure solids?

Insta-Lab

**Sort Classroom Objects**

With a partner, gather some classroom objects. Take turns naming their properties. Then sort the objects in different ways. Did you sort by color, by shape, by size, by how much they weigh, or by texture?

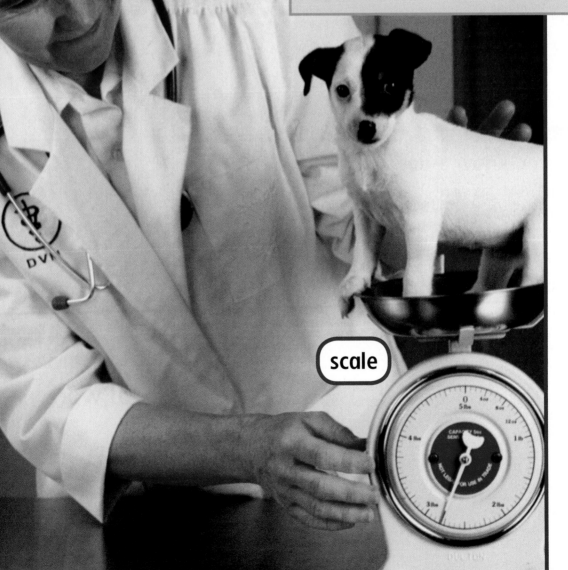

scale

**What can we observe about solids?**

In this lesson, you learned that a solid takes up space and has mass. A solid keeps its shape.

**Science Content Standards in This Lesson**

**I.a** *Students know* solids, liquids, and gases have different properties.

**1.** **Focus Skill MAIN IDEA AND DETAILS**
Make a chart like this one. Show details of this main idea. **A solid is matter that keeps its shape.** I.a

Main Idea
detail  detail  detail

**2.** **DRAW CONCLUSIONS** How do you know a desk is a solid? I.a

**3.** **VOCABULARY** Use the word **solid** to tell about these blocks. I.a

**4.** **Critical Thinking** Think of a solid object. What are some ways you could measure it? Write a plan. I.a

**5.** Which of these is a solid? I.a
**A** air
**B** car
**C** milk
**D** water

## The Big Idea

**6.** What are some properties of a solid? I.a

### Writing  ELA– WS 2.2

## Write to Describe

1. Write riddles about three solid objects in the classroom.

2. Read your riddles aloud.

3. Ask your classmates to guess what your objects are.

I am a solid.

I can spin.

Names of places are written on me.

What am I?

Answer: a globe

### Math  MG 1.1, SDAP 1.2

## Measure Length

1. Find three small objects in your classroom.

2. Use paper clips to measure how long they are.

3. Record in a bar graph how long they are.

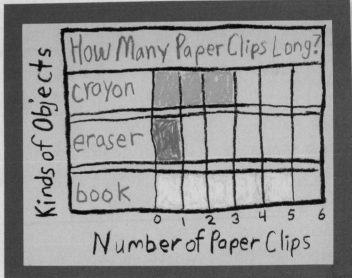

How Many Paper Clips Long?

Kinds of Objects

crayon

eraser

book

0 1 2 3 4 5 6

Number of Paper Clips

For more links and activities, go to **www.hspscience.com**

## Science Content

**1.a** *Students know* solids, liquids, and gases have different properties.

## Investigation and Experimentation

**4.a** Draw pictures that portray some features of the thing being described.

**4.c** Record observations on a bar graph.

Essential Question

# What Can We Observe About Liquids?

## California Fast Fact

### Los Angeles Fire Boats

Fire boats are like fire trucks, but they float on water. They help firefighters put out fires. Fire boats use water to put out fires on boats. They also put out fires on other things near or in the water.

**liquid** p. 77

**float** p. 78

**sink** p. 79

**Los Angeles City Fire Department Fire Boat**

# The Shape of Liquids

## Ask a Question

If you pour juice into these containers, how will the shape of the juice change?

## Get Ready

**Investigation Skill Tip**
When you predict, you use what you know to make a guess about what will happen.

**You need**

3 containers of water

measuring cup

# What to Do

**Step ①**

Look at the containers.
Draw their shapes.

**Step ②**

**Predict** which container
has the most water in it.

**Step ③**

Measure the water in
each container. Was your
prediction correct?

## Draw Conclusions

What did you find out
about the properties of
liquids? `1.a`

---

**Independent Inquiry**

Get different balls.
**Predict** whether each
ball will float or sink.
Then check. Record your
answers on a bar
graph. `4.c`

**VOCABULARY**
liquid
float
sink

**Focus Skill MAIN IDEA AND DETAILS**

Look for the main ideas about liquids.

# Properties of Liquids

How are the soap and the water the same? They are both liquids.

liquid soap

water

If you pour a liquid from one container into another, its shape changes. The amount of liquid stays the same.

A **liquid** is matter that flows. It does not have its own shape. It takes the shape of its container. You can see and feel a liquid. It takes up space. It also has mass.

(Focus Skill) **MAIN IDEA AND DETAILS** Why does a liquid take the shape of its container?

# Float and Sink

Which objects float? Which sink? You can test them to find out.

Some solids **float**, or stay on top of a liquid.

Which objects float?

Some solids **sink**, or fall to the bottom of a liquid.

**Focus Skill** **MAIN IDEA AND DETAILS** What are some objects that float?

Which objects sink?

**Insta-Lab**

**What Floats?**
Get a coin, a pencil, and other small classroom objects. Predict which ones will float. Put each object into a large bowl of water. Were your predictions correct?

# Measuring Liquids

You can measure liquids. You can use a measuring cup to find out how much space a liquid takes up.

measuring cup

balance

You can also use a balance to measure liquids. You use a balance to measure the mass of a liquid.

**Focus Skill MAIN IDEA AND DETAILS** How can you measure liquids?

## Essential Question

**What can we observe about liquids?**

In this lesson, you learned that a liquid takes up space and has mass. A liquid flows to take the shape of its container.

**Science Content Standards in This Lesson**

**1.a** *Students know* solids, liquids, and gases have different properties.

---

**1.** (Focus Skill) **MAIN IDEA AND DETAILS**
Make a chart like this one. Identify the main idea and details about liquids.  **1.a**

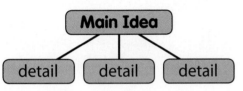

Main Idea

detail   detail   detail

**2. SUMMARIZE** Tell what you have learned about the properties of liquids.  **1.a**

**3.** VOCABULARY Use **sink** and **float** to tell about this picture.  **1.a**

---

**4. Investigation** You drew the shapes of the containers in the Investigate. How did that help you make a prediction?  **4.a**

**5.** Which tool would you use to measure the mass of a liquid?  **1.a**
A  a balance
B  a hand lens
C  a measuring cup
D  a ruler

## The **Big Idea**

**6.** Tell about the properties of this liquid.  **1.a**

### Writing
ELA– WS 2.2

## Write to Inform

1. Choose your favorite kind of liquid to drink.

2. Draw the shape of the container the liquid comes in.

3. Write sentences telling about the liquid and why you like it.

Milk is white.
It comes from cows.
I like it because it tastes good.

### Math
MG 1.0

## Measure Liquids

1. Find two small containers in your classroom.

2. Predict how many bottle caps of water it will take to fill up each container.

3. Use the bottle caps to fill each container with water. Was your prediction correct?

For more links and activities, go to **www.hspscience.com**

## Science Content

**1.a** *Students know* solids, liquids, and gases have different properties.

## Investigation and Experimentation

**4.b** Record observations and data with pictures, numbers, or written statements.

Essential Question

# What Can We Observe About Gases?

## California Fast Fact

**Temecula Valley Balloon Festival**

Hot-air balloons rise. The warm air inside a balloon is lighter than the cool air around it. The balloons move as fast as the wind is blowing.

**gas** p. 88

Temecula Valley
Balloon Festival

# Matter in a Bottle

## Ask a Question

These balloons have been made into the shapes of animals. What shape does the air take in each balloon?

## Get Ready

**Investigation Skill Tip**
When you infer, you use what you observed to tell why something happened.

### You need

clean plastic bottle

balloon

## What to Do

**Step 1**

Squeeze the bottle. Blow up the balloon and hold it loosely. Observe the air coming out of each.

**Step 2**

Put the balloon in the bottle. Pull the end around the top. Try to blow up the balloon.

**Step 3**

Write what you observe. **Infer** what else is in the bottle.

## Draw Conclusions

What did you find out about gases? 1.a

**Independent Inquiry**

Mix yeast, sugar, and water in a zip-top plastic bag. Zip the bag shut. **Infer** what happens inside the bag. 4.b

(Focus Skill) **MAIN IDEA AND DETAILS**

Look for the main ideas about gases.

# Properties of Gases

A **gas** is matter that does not have its own shape. It takes the shape of its container. It spreads out to fill all of its container. A gas takes up space and has mass.

**Where is the gas in each picture?**

88

Air is made of gases. It is all around you. Often you can not see, smell, or feel air. You can see and feel what air does as it moves.

★ Focus Skill **MAIN IDEA AND DETAILS** **What would happen if you blew air into a bag? Explain.**

Air that moves makes a kite fly.

## Insta-Lab

### A Wind Hunt

Did you know that wind is air that is moving? Go on an air hunt. Tape yarn to a pencil. Have an adult turn on an air conditioner, a fan, or a hair dryer. Hold the pencil near it. Observe the yarn. What makes it move?

# Measuring Gases

You can measure to find out
how much space a gas takes up.

You can use a balance to measure the mass of a gas.

**Focus Skill** **MAIN IDEA AND DETAILS** What are two ways you can measure a gas?

Which balloon has more mass? Explain.

# Standards Wrap-Up and Lesson Review

**What can we observe about gases?**

In this lesson, you learned that a gas takes up space and has mass. A gas takes the shape of its container.

 **Science Content Standards in This Lesson**

**I.a** *Students know* solids, liquids, and gases have different properties.

1. (Focus Skill) **MAIN IDEA AND DETAILS**
   Make a chart like this one. Use the chart to write what you have learned about gases. **I.a**

   ```
            Main Idea
        /      |      \
   detail   detail   detail
   ```

2. **DRAW CONCLUSIONS** Is ice a gas? Tell how you know. **I.a**

3. **VOCABULARY** Use the word **gas** to tell about this picture. **I.a**

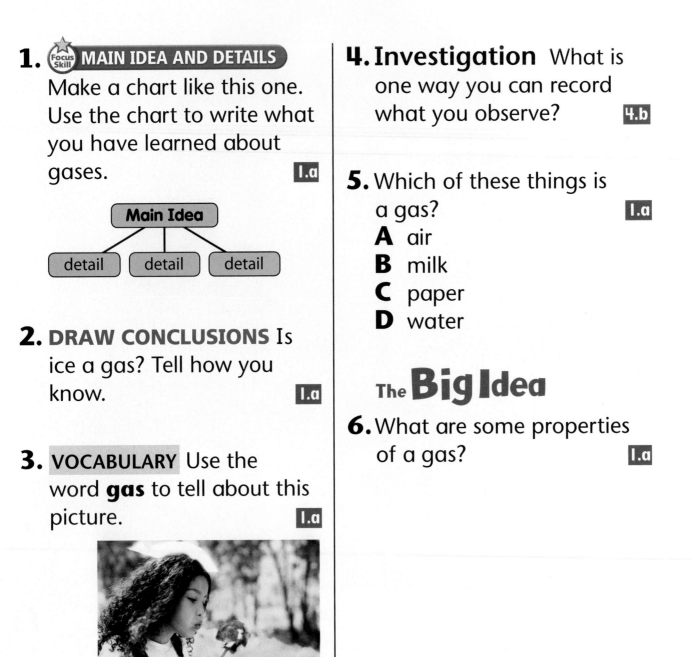

4. **Investigation** What is one way you can record what you observe? **4.b**

5. Which of these things is a gas? **I.a**
   A air
   B milk
   C paper
   D water

## The Big Idea

6. What are some properties of a gas? **I.a**

**Writing**     ELA–WS 2.1

## Write a Story

1. Write a story about the differences between the properties of solids, liquids, and gases.

2. Draw pictures to go with your story.

3. Share your writing with the class.

Gas spreads out to fill its container.

**Math**     MG 1.1

## Measure a Gas

1. Put a balloon filled with air on one side of a balance.

2. Put a balloon without air on the other side.

3. Compare their masses.

4. Record what you observe.

For more links and activities, go to **www.hspscience.com**

**RONALD FEARING**

▶ California Engineer

▶ Works to make a new kind of glue

# Ronald Fearing

Would it be useful to have a robot that could climb walls? This may soon be possible—thanks to geckos!

Ronald Fearing watched these little lizards hang by just one toe. He saw them climb smooth glass. He saw them run across a ceiling. How did they do it? Fearing studied their feet to find out. Millions of tiny hairs make gecko feet sticky. Now Ronald Fearing and others are working to make a new kind of glue. It will work the way the hairs on a gecko's feet do.

## Think and Write

Why was it important for Ronald Fearing to carefully observe gecko feet?

gecko foot

gecko

# Joseph Priestley

Joseph Priestley was a scientist. He worked on learning more about gases. He and another scientist were the first to discover oxygen. Joseph Priestley was the first to show that fire needs oxygen to burn. He also discovered how to use a gas to make water fizzy. Joseph Priestley made the world's first glass of soda water!

**JOSEPH PRIESTLEY**
▶ Chemist
▶ Discovered oxygen and other gases

## Think and Write

Why is it important to know that fire needs oxygen to burn?

soda water

## Science Content

**1.b** *Students know* the properties of substances can change when the substances are mixed, cooled, or heated.

## Investigation and Experimentation

**4.b** Record observations and data with pictures, numbers, or written statements.

Essential Question

# How Can Matter Change?

## California Fast Fact

**Tioga Lake**

From Tioga Lake you can see Yosemite National Park. During the winter, the lake freezes.

**mixture** p. 100

**freeze** p. 102

**melt** p. 104

Tioga Lake

97

# Make a Mixture

## Ask a Question

The things in a mixture do not change when you put them together. How is this salad a mixture?

## Get Ready

**Investigation Skill Tip**
You can use pictures, numbers, or writing to tell what you observe.

**You need**

dried fruits and seeds

measuring cup

zip-top bag

## What to Do

**Step 1**

Measure the same amounts of dried fruits and seeds.

**Step 2**

Put the foods into the bag. Zip the bag shut, and then shake it.

**Step 3**

Record what you observe. Write sentences to **tell** what you see.

## Draw Conclusions

What things changed? What things stayed the same? **1.b**

**Independent Inquiry**

Separate the foods in the mixture. Do they look the same as they did when they were in the mixture? **Tell** what you see. **4.b**

**VOCABULARY**
mixture
freeze
melt

**CAUSE AND EFFECT**

Look for ways matter can change. Find the cause of each change.

# Mixing Matter

You make a **mixture** when you mix two or more kinds of matter. This fruit salad is a mixture. You can take the mixture apart. Each piece will be the same shape and size as it was in the mixture.

fruit salad

lemonade

Lemonade is a mixture. You mix water, lemon juice, and sugar to make it. The water turns yellow. You can not see the sugar.

The sugar mixes with the liquid. The mixture tastes sweet. If you heat the liquid, it becomes a gas. Then you can see the sugar again.

**Focus Skill CAUSE AND EFFECT** What happens to fruit pieces when you mix them?

**Insta-Lab**

**Mix It Up**

Mix four spoonfuls of cornstarch with two spoonfuls of water. Roll the mixture in your hands. Pour it from hand to hand. What happens?

# Freezing

Water changes to ice when you cool it. It **freezes**, or changes from a liquid to a solid. Ice has the properties of a solid.

The tray is filled with liquid juice. Juice is mostly water. How will it change when it freezes?

The frozen juice is not a liquid now. It is an ice pop. It has its own shape.

**Focus Skill CAUSE AND EFFECT** What caused the juice to change from a liquid to a solid?

liquid

solid

# Melting

Warm air is adding heat to the ice. The ice pop is melting. To **melt** is to change from a solid to a liquid.

melting ice pop

The melted ice pop is not a solid now. It is juice again. It does not have its own shape.

**Focus Skill** **CAUSE AND EFFECT** Why did the ice pop melt?

liquid

# Evaporation

The water in this pot is changing to a gas. Water changes when you add heat to it. It evaporates, or changes from a liquid to a gas. You can not see the gas in the air. It has the properties of a gas.

**Focus Skill** **CAUSE AND EFFECT** What causes water to change to a gas?

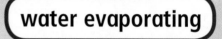

water evaporating

## What Is Steam?

When water boils, it becomes a gas called steam.

**1** When the water gets hot enough, it becomes steam. The steam goes into the air.

**2** As steam cools, it forms tiny drops of water that make a little cloud.

For more links and animations, go to **www.hspscience.com**

**107**

## Essential Question

### How can matter change?

In this lesson, you learned that properties of matter can change when you mix, heat, or cool it.

 **Science Content Standards in This Lesson**

**I.b** *Students know* the properties of substances can change when the substances are mixed, cooled, or heated.

**1.** (Focus Skill) **CAUSE AND EFFECT** Make a chart like this one. Show what causes some changes in matter. **I.b**

cause ⟶ effect

**2.** **SUMMARIZE** Use the chart to write a summary of this lesson. **I.b**

**3.** **VOCABULARY** Use the word **freeze** to tell about this picture. **I.b**

**4.** **Critical Thinking** Can ice that becomes a liquid change back to a solid? Explain. **I.b**

**5.** Which word means to change from a solid to a liquid? **I.b**
**A** freeze
**B** gas
**C** liquid
**D** melt

## The Big Idea

**6.** List ways properties of matter change if you mix, heat, or cool it. **I.b**

### Writing
ELA–WS 2.2

## Write to Inform

1. Write a few sentences about mixtures you ate for lunch.

2. Draw pictures to go with your writing.

3. Share your writing and pictures with the class.

I can take the meatballs out of the spaghetti.

### Math
NS 1.2

## Measure and Compare

1. Measure the temperature of a cup of water.

2. Then measure the temperature of a cup of ice.

3. Use >, <, or = to compare the two temperatures.

For more links and activities, go to **www.hspscience.com**

# Cleaning Up Oil

Oil is a thick liquid.

Oil spills can happen when a boat carrying oil hits something. Oil is liquid that does not mix with water. It floats on water.

oil tanker

Oil pollutes water in oceans, lakes, and rivers. It also hurts animals. Scientists have worked to find ways to clean up oil spills.

When oil gets into the ocean, it is very hard to clean up. Workers must use special soap and sponges to clean up the oil.

## Think and Write

How can oil spills hurt the environment?

Find out more. Log on to **www.hspscience.com**

## Science Content

**1.b** *Students know* the properties of substances can change when the substances are mixed, cooled, or heated.

## Investigation and Experimentation

**4.a** Draw pictures that portray some features of the thing being described.

LESSON

# 6

Essential Question

# What Are Other Changes to Matter?

## California Fast Fact

### Gilroy Garlic Festival

Gilroy is the garlic capital of the world. At the festival, chefs cook foods with garlic over large fire pits.

Gilroy Garlic Festival

**burn** p. 117

**113**

# Changing Matter

## Ask a Question

This pizza was cooked. How did the matter change?

## Get Ready

**Investigation Skill Tip**
When you observe, you use your senses to find out about things. You can use pictures to record what you see.

### You need

toaster

bread

## What to Do

**Step ①**

**Observe** a piece of bread. Draw what you see.

**Step ②**

Ask your teacher to toast the bread.

**Step ③**

Observe the bread again. Draw what you see now. What changed?

## Draw Conclusions

What caused the bread to change? `1.b`

**Independent Inquiry**

**Observe** some uncooked popcorn. Ask your teacher to pop it. Then observe the popcorn again. How did it change? `4.a`

**VOCABULARY**
burn

**Focus Skill** **CAUSE AND EFFECT**

Look for the causes and effects of changes from burning and cooking.

# Burning

Fire changes matter into new matter. The new matter can not change back into what it was before.

The fire is changing this wood. It **burns** the wood, or changes it to ashes and smoke. The ashes and smoke can not change back into wood.

Focus Skill **CAUSE AND EFFECT** What causes wood to change to ashes and smoke?

## Cooking

Cooking also changes matter into new matter. The light brown bread changes to dark brown toast. It also gets harder. It can not change back to the way it was before it was cooked.

uncooked bread

cooked toast

The eggs also change. Their color, size, shape, and texture change. They can never be uncooked eggs again.

**Focus Skill CAUSE AND EFFECT** How do the eggs change because they are cooked?

uncooked eggs

cooked eggs

## Insta-Lab

**Uncooked and Cooked**
Draw pictures to show what pasta looks like before and after it is cooked. How do the pasta's properties change?

# Making Muffins

You cook a mixture when you make muffins. The properties of the mixture change when it is cooked. Its size, shape, color, and texture change.

**1** Mix the ingredients.

**2** Pour the mixture into a muffin pan.

For more links and animations, go to www.hspscience.com

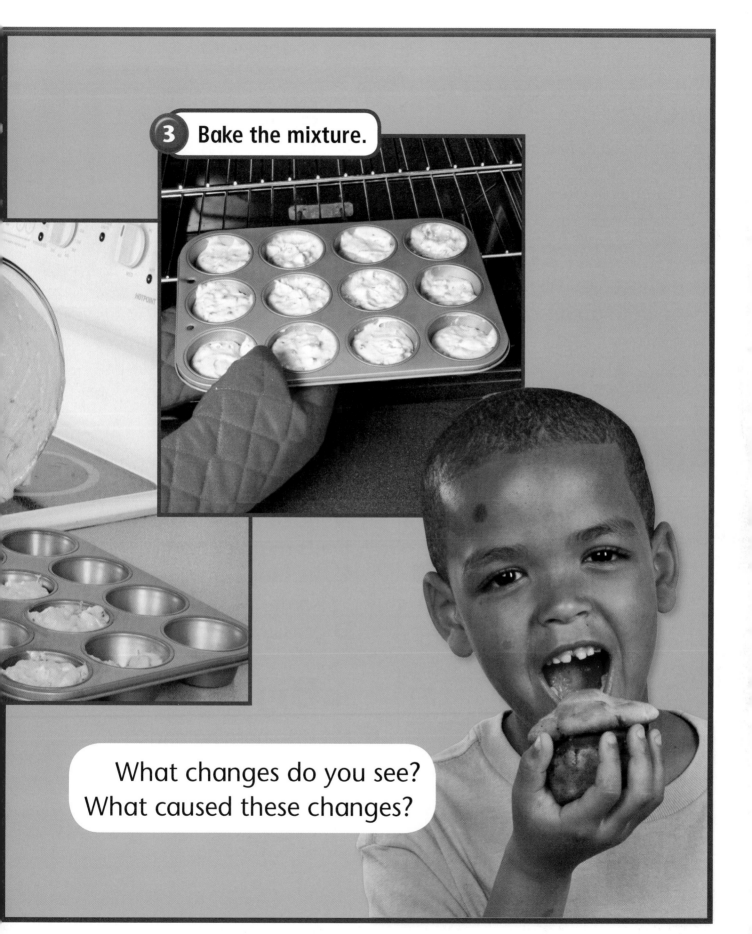

3 Bake the mixture.

What changes do you see?
What caused these changes?

121

**Essential Question**

### What are other changes to matter?

In this lesson, you learned that the properties of matter change when you burn it or cook it.

 **Science Content Standards in This Lesson**

**I.b** *Students know* the properties of substances can change when the substances are mixed, cooled, or heated.

**1.**  **CAUSE AND EFFECT** Make a chart like this one. Use it to write about changes in matter. **I.b**

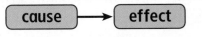

**2. DRAW CONCLUSIONS** Can a cooked piece of meat change back to an uncooked piece of meat? Explain. **I.b**

**3. VOCABULARY** Use the word **burn** to tell about this picture. **I.b**

**4. Investigation** In the Investigate, you drew the bread and then the toast. How did drawing them help you observe the changes? **4.a**

**5.** What happens when paper burns? **I.b**
   **A** Its color stays the same.
   **B** Its matter changes.
   **C** Its shape stays the same.
   **D** Its size stays the same.

### The Big Idea

**6.** How do burning and cooking change the properties of matter? **I.b**

**Writing** 🐻 ELA–WS 2.2

### Write to Inform

1. Work with a partner. Make two lists of foods.

2. In one list, write the names of foods that have to be cooked. In the other list, write the names of foods that do not have to be cooked.

3. Tell how cooking changes food.

| Have to Be Cooked | Do Not Have to Be Cooked |
| --- | --- |
| eggs | apples |
| pancakes | tomatoes |
| bacon | carrots |

**Math** 🐻 SDAP 1.2

### Measuring Temperature

1. Use four thermometers. Put them inside a white sock, a black sock, a red sock, and a yellow sock. Lay the socks in the sun for 5 minutes.

2. Then record the four temperatures. Make a bar graph to compare them.

For more links and activities, go to **www.hspscience.com**

123

# The Children's Discovery Museum of San Jose

The Children's Discovery Museum of San Jose is one of the biggest children's museums in the United States. One part of it is called WaterWays. In WaterWays, you can find out how water flows. You can also learn how a fountain works.

San Jose

Another part of the museum is called Bubbalogna. If you like bubbles, you will love Bubbalogna! You can see the way bubbles catch light.

At the Children's Discovery Museum of San Jose, you can touch things, test things, and play with things. Where would you like to start?

Bubbalogna

✎ **Think and Write**
What shape is the air inside the bubbles? I.a

WaterWays

125

# Wrap-Up

## ▶Visual Summary

Tell how each picture helps explain the **Big Idea**.

**The Big Idea** Matter has different states. Three of the states are solid, liquid, and gas.

**1.a**

Solids, liquids, and gases have different properties. A solid keeps its shape when you move it. Liquids and gases do not have their own shapes. A liquid takes the shape of its container. A gas fills up all of its container.

**1.b**

Properties of things can change when they are mixed, cooled, or heated. Water is a liquid. It changes to ice when it freezes. Ice is a solid. It changes to water when it melts.

# Show What You Know

## Write How to Make a Healthful Snack

A mixture of cereal, nuts, and raisins is a healthful snack. Use different amounts of each food. Put the foods together in different ways. Which way do you like the best? Write directions for how to make the snack.

## Unit Project

### Record Data About Matter

For two weeks, record the solids, liquids, and gases you see at school. Each day, write about or draw what you see. Compare your list with the lists your classmates made. Work together to make a class bulletin board. Show the matter you saw.

Solids    Liquids    Gases

## Vocabulary Review

Use the words to complete the sentences. The page numbers tell you where to look if you need help.

**matter** p. 56        **solid** p. 67

**property** p. 58      **liquid** p. 77

**mass** p. 58          **gas** p. 88

**1.** A _____ is something that always keeps its own shape.        `1.a`

**2.** A _____ is something that spreads out to fill all of its container.        `1.a`

**3.** A _____ is something that takes the shape of its container.        `1.a`

**4.** Solids, liquids, and gases are all forms of _____.        `1.a`

**5.** One part of what something is like is a _____ of the thing.        `1.a`

**6.** The _____ of something is how much matter it has.        `1.a`

# Check Understanding

**7.** Which picture shows a mixture? `1.b`

**8.** What may cause a solid to melt? `1.b`

**A** cooling it

**B** freezing it

**C** heating it

**D** mixing it

# Critical Thinking

**9.** When water is cooled a lot, it freezes. How is this different from the change that takes place when an egg is cooked? `1.b`

## The **Big Idea**

**10.** How are solids, liquids, and gases alike? How are they different?

# Plants and Animals Meet Their Needs

**What's the Big Idea?**

Plants and animals need some things to live and grow. They meet their needs in different ways.

## Essential Questions

Sacramento

Dear Dava,

   Our class went to the Sacramento Zoo. We learned that an animal's teeth show what kind of food it eats. A zebra has flat teeth that help it eat plants.

Your friend,

Luis

Read Luis's postcard. What did Luis learn about zebras? How do you think that helps explain the **Big Idea?**

**Unit Inquiry**

## Plants and Light
**How does light change the way plants grow? Plan and do a test to find out.**

## Science Content

**2.b** *Students know* both plants and animals need water, animals need food, and plants need light.

**2.e** *Students know* roots are associated with the intake of water and soil nutrients and green leaves are associated with making food from sunlight.

## Investigation and Experimentation

**4.b** Record observations and data with pictures, numbers, or written statements.

**Essential Question**

# What Do Plants Need?

## California Fast Fact

### The General Sherman Tree

The General Sherman Tree is the largest living thing in the world. It is 84 meters (276 feet) tall. That is about as tall as a 25-story building!

## Vocabulary Preview

**roots** p. 140

**leaves** p. 141

the General
Sherman Tree

**133**

# Predict What Plants Will Need

## Ask a Question

How would you take care of this plant?

## Get Ready

**Investigation Skill Tip**
When you predict, you use what you know to guess what will happen.

### You need

index cards

2 small plants

spray bottle with water

134

## What to Do

**Step ➊**

Label the plants. Put both plants in a sunny place.

**Step ➋**

Water only one of the plants. **Predict** what will happen to each plant.

**Step ➌**

After four days, check the plants. Draw or write to record what you see. Was your prediction correct?

## Draw Conclusions

What did you find out about the needs of plants?  2.b

**Independent Inquiry**

Measure a young plant. Record the number. **Predict** how tall the plant will be in two weeks.  4.b

**VOCABULARY**
roots
leaves

⭐ (Focus Skill) **MAIN IDEA AND DETAILS**

Look for all the things that plants need to grow and stay healthy.

# Light, Air, and Water

A plant needs things to grow and stay healthy. A plant needs light, air, and water to make food. It also needs water to move the food to all its parts.

sunlight

air

water

Plants take in sunlight, or light from the sun. They take in water, too. They get most of the water from the soil.

**Focus Skill** **MAIN IDEA AND DETAILS** What things do plants need to make food?

# Soil

Plants take in water and nutrients from the soil. Water and nutrients help plants grow.

**(Focus Skill) MAIN IDEA AND DETAILS** Why does a plant need soil?

soil

**flower**

## Parts of a Plant

Plants have different parts. The parts help the plant live and grow. Most plants have roots, a stem, and leaves. Some plants have flowers.

**stem**

**leaf**

**roots**

For more links and animations, go to **www.hspscience.com**

# Roots

The **roots** hold the plant in the soil. They also take in the water and nutrients that the plant needs.

**Focus Skill: MAIN IDEA AND DETAILS**

What are two ways that roots help plants?

Where are the roots on these plants?

# Leaves

**Leaves** take in light and air. They use these things to make food for the plant. The leaves of different kinds of plants look different.

What shapes do these leaves have?

# Standards Wrap-Up and Lesson Review

## Essential Question

### What do plants need?

In this lesson, you learned that plants need light, air, and water. You also learned that roots and leaves help plants get what they need.

## Science Content Standards in This Lesson

**2.b** *Students know* that both plants and animals need water, animals need food, and plants need light.

**2.e** *Students know* roots are associated with the intake of water and soil nutrients and green leaves are associated with making food from sunlight.

**1.** (Focus Skill) **MAIN IDEA AND DETAILS**
Make a chart like this one. Show details of this main idea. **A plant needs things to grow and stay healthy**. **2.b, 2.e**

```
        Main Idea
       /    |    \
 detail  detail  detail
```

**2. SUMMARIZE** Use the vocabulary words to write a lesson summary. **2.b, 2.e**

**3. VOCABULARY**
Use the words **roots** and **leaves** to tell about this picture. **2.e**

**4. Investigation** In the Investigate, you recorded what you saw. How did this help you decide if your prediction was correct? **4.b**

**5.** Which part of a plant makes the food? **2.e**
**A** flower
**B** leaves
**C** roots
**D** stem

## The Big Idea

**6.** What things does a plant need? How do roots and leaves help it meet its needs? **2.b, 2.e**

**Writing**  ELA–WS 1.0

## Write How-To Take Care of Plants

1. What could you do for a plant that does not look healthy? Write a plan.

2. Draw a picture to show your plan.

3. Share your plan and your drawing with the rest of the class.

**Math**  MG 1.1

## Measuring Leaves

1. Put some leaves under a sheet of paper.

2. Rub the paper over the leaves with the sides of crayons.

3. Use small blocks to measure the rubbings. Record how long each leaf is.

For more links and activities, go to **www.hspscience.com**

## Science Content

**2.b** *Students know* both plants and animals need water, animals need food, and plants need light.

**2.d** *Students know* how to infer what animals eat from the shape of their teeth (e.g., sharp teeth: eats meat; flat teeth: eats plants).

## Investigation and Experimentation

**4.b** Record observations and data with pictures, numbers, or written statements.

**Essential Question**

# What Do Animals Need?

## California Fast Fact

### California Bighorn Sheep

Male bighorn sheep are called rams. The rams grow very large horns that curl. You can count the rings on a horn to see how old the ram is.

**shelter** p. 153

bighorn sheep

# Observe an Animal Home

**Directed Inquiry**

## Ask a Question

What do these animals need to live and grow?

## Get Ready

**Investigation Skill Tip**
When you observe, you use your senses to find out about things. You can draw pictures to record what you see.

### You need

plastic box and gloves

soil, twig, leaf, rocks

water in a bottle cap

small animals

## What to Do

**Step ①**

Put the soil, twig, leaf, rocks, and water in the box. Add the animals.

**Step ②**

**Observe.** Draw pictures to record what you see.

**Step ③**

Tell how the home that you made gives the animals food, water, and a place to live.

## Draw Conclusions

What did you find out about the needs of animals?

 2.b

**Independent Inquiry**

Go for a nature walk. **Observe** how animals meet their needs. Record what you observe. 4.b

**Focus Skill** **MAIN IDEA AND DETAILS**

Look for all the things that animals need to live.

# Animals Need Food and Water

Animals need food to live and to grow. Animals can not make their own food. They have to find it. An elephant eats grasses, branches, and fruits.

Animals need water, too. Elephants drink from ponds. They also get water from the foods that they eat.

**Focus Skill MAIN IDEA AND DETAILS** What are two things that animals need to live?

**Pet Food Survey**

Take a survey. List some pet foods. Then ask your classmates what their pets eat. Make a tally mark next to each food. Which food do the most pets eat?

A panda eats bamboo.

A horse drinks water from a pond.

# Animal Teeth

You can tell what kind of food an animal eats. You can do this by looking at its teeth. Some animals eat plants. These animals have flat teeth. They use their teeth for chewing plants.

A cow eats grass.

A cow has flat teeth for chewing and grinding grass.

A cheetah eats other animals.

A cheetah has sharp, pointed teeth for biting and tearing meat.

Some animals eat other animals. These animals have sharp, pointed teeth. They use their teeth for biting and tearing meat.

**Focus Skill** **MAIN IDEA AND DETAILS** How can you tell what kind of food an animal eats?

# Animals Need Air

All animals need air. They have body parts that help them get air. Lungs help some animals take in air. A porcupine has lungs. Some animals, such as fish, have gills. Gills take air from water.

fish

**(Focus Skill) MAIN IDEA AND DETAILS** What are two body parts animals use to get air?

porcupine

# Animals Need Shelter

Most animals need shelter. A **shelter** is a place where an animal can be safe. Some birds use trees as shelters. Foxes dig holes in the ground for shelter.

**(Focus Skill) MAIN IDEA AND DETAILS** What is a shelter?

owl

foxes

## Essential Question

**What do animals need?**

In this lesson, you learned that animals need food, water, air, and shelter. You also learned that some animals have sharp teeth and some have flat teeth.

### Science Content Standards in This Lesson

**2.b** *Students know* both plants and animals need water, animals need food, and plants need light.

**2.d** *Students know* how to infer what animals eat from the shape of their teeth (e.g., sharp teeth: eats meat; flat teeth: eats plants).

1. **MAIN IDEA AND DETAILS**
   Make a chart like this one. Tell the things animals need to live and grow. **2.b**

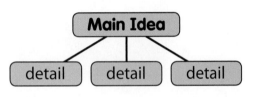

2. **DRAW CONCLUSIONS**
   What are some body parts animals use to meet their needs? **2.d**

3. **VOCABULARY** Use the word **shelter** to tell about this picture. **2.b**

4. **Critical Thinking** Draw a picture of a pet you would like to have. List the things it would need. Tell how you would help it meet its needs. **2.b**

5. What do lungs and gills help animals get? **2.b**
   A air
   B food
   C shelter
   D water

## The Big Idea

6. List four things animals need. Tell how you can infer what an animal eats by looking at the shape of its teeth. **2.b, 2.d**

## Writing  ELA–WS 2.2

### Write to Inform

1. Use a mirror to look at your teeth.

2. Write about which teeth you use to eat different foods.

3. Share your writing with the rest of the class.

I use my front teeth to bite an apple.

## Math  NS 2.7, AF 1.0

### Compare Amounts

1. Different animals need different amounts of food. Use the chart to compare how much food three dogs eat each day.

2. Which eats the most? The least? How much would each dog eat in 3 days?

| Dog | Amount of Food |
|-----|----------------|
| Sandy | 1 cup |
| Rosey | 2 cups |
| Bo | 3 cups |

For more links and activities, go to **www.hspscience.com**

### Science Content

**2.a** *Students know* different plants and animals inhabit different kinds of environments and have external features that help them thrive in different kinds of places.

### Investigation and Experimentation

**4.b** Record observations and data with pictures, numbers, or written statements.

**Essential Question**

# Where Do Plants and Animals Live?

## California Fast Fact

### California Sea Lions

Sea lions live in the ocean. They have a thick layer of blubber, or fat. The blubber keeps them warm in the cold ocean.

**forest** p. 164

**desert** p. 166

**ocean** p. 168

sea lions

157

# Some Animals Hide

## Ask a Question

How are the colors of these animals helping them hide?

dead-leaf butterfly

frog

## Get Ready

**Investigation Skill Tip**
When you observe, you use your senses to find out about things. You can use pictures, numbers, or words to record what you see.

## You need

colored paper clips

colored paper

arctic fox

## What to Do

**Step 1**

Put the clips on a sheet of colored paper. **Observe.** Record what you see.

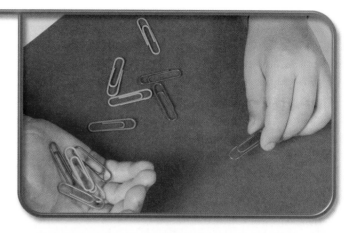

**Step 2**

Put the clips on a sheet of paper of a different color. Observe. Record what you see now.

**Step 3**

Compare what you see with what a classmate sees.

## Draw Conclusions

What did you find out about how some animals' colors help them hide? **2.a**

**Independent Inquiry**

Think about what living things need. **Draw a conclusion** about what you need. What body parts help you get the things you need? **4.b**

**VOCABULARY**
forest
desert
ocean

⭐ **MAIN IDEA AND DETAILS**

Look for the main ideas about where plants and animals live.

# How Plants Change

Plants have changed over time so they can live in different environments. The changes help them meet their needs.

Water lilies grow in a pond. Their leaves float on the water. The leaves get the sunlight they need.

water lilies

A jade plant has thick leaves that store water. These plants can live in dry places.

A banyan tree has many roots. The roots help hold up the tree. These trees can spread out very wide without falling.

Focus Skill **MAIN IDEA AND DETAILS**

**What are some plant parts that help plants live in their environments?**

jade plant

banyan tree

# How Animals Change

Animals have also changed over time so they can live in different environments. These changes help them meet their needs.

Sea otters have thick fur. Whales have thick skin. These animals can live in cold water.

whales

sea otters

Giraffes live on flat land where there are trees. Giraffes have long necks that help them reach leaves near the tops of trees. Their long necks also help them see danger from far away. This helps keep giraffes safe.

**(Focus Skill) MAIN IDEA AND DETAILS** What are some body parts that help animals live in their environments?

giraffe

## Science Up Close

# Camouflage

Some animals have camouflage. Camouflage is a color or pattern that helps an animal hide. It helps the animal stay safe or get food.

flounder

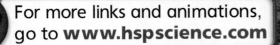
For more links and animations, go to **www.hspscience.com**

# Forest Plants

A **forest** is land covered with trees. In a forest, trees get enough rain and sun to grow tall. They have long trunks. Their leaves can get the light they need to make food. Ferns and flowers grow on the forest floor. They have short stems. These plants need water, but they do not need as much light as trees need.

(Focus Skill) **MAIN IDEA AND DETAILS** Why do some plants live in forests?

wildflowers

ferns

# Forest Animals

Many animals live in forests. They have body parts that help them find food, water, and shelter there.

An eagle lives in a forest. It can see food from high in the air. It has claws that help it catch and carry its food.

**MAIN IDEA AND DETAILS** Why do some animals live in a forest?

How are these animals meeting their needs?

bear

eagle

skunk

165

# Desert Plants

A **desert** is a place that gets very little rain. Most deserts are sunny all year long. Desert plants do not need much water.

A cactus is a desert plant. It can hold water in its thick stem. Its waxy covering keeps in the water.

**Focus Skill** **MAIN IDEA AND DETAILS** How does a cactus live without much water?

creosote

brittlebush

cactus

# Desert Animals

Desert animals need to keep cool and find water. The dove and the hare rest in shady places. The tortoise gets water from its food.

**Focus Skill** **MAIN IDEA AND DETAILS** What are two needs that desert animals have?

white-winged dove

A desert hare has large ears. They help keep the hare cool.

How are these animals meeting their needs?

desert tortoise

# Oceans

An **ocean** is a large body of salt water. Oceans cover much of Earth.

Kelp and other seaweeds grow in the ocean. Their long leaves reach up to get the sunlight they need.

sea otter

stingray

sea lion

Ocean animals live where they can find food. Sea lions eat fish and squid. The shape of a sea lion's body lets it dive deep to find food.

Sea turtles have large flippers. Stingrays have body parts shaped like wings. These animals use these parts to swim hundreds of miles to find food.

**Focus Skill** **MAIN IDEA AND DETAILS** **Where do ocean animals live?**

sea turtle

kelp

# Standards Wrap-Up and Lesson Review

## Essential Question

### Where do plants and animals live?

In this lesson, you learned that some plants and animals live in forests, deserts, and oceans. You also learned why they can live where they do.

 **Science Content Standards in This Lesson**

**2.a** *Students know* different plants and animals inhabit different kinds of environments and have external features that help them thrive in different kinds of places.

---

**1.** (Focus Skill) **MAIN IDEA AND DETAILS**
Make a chart like this one. Tell where plants and animals live. **2.a**

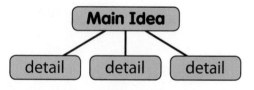

**2. SUMMARIZE** What is this lesson about? Write a summary. **2.a**

**3.** VOCABULARY Use the word **desert** to tell about this animal. **2.a**

**4. Critical Thinking** You can find many of this kind of plant in a forest. It needs rain and sun. It grows tall so its leaves get light. What kind of plant is it? **2.a**

**5.** What do flippers help a sea turtle do? **2.a**
**A** keep cool
**B** rest in shade
**C** swim to find food
**D** store water

## The **Big Idea**

**6.** Think of three environments. Name some plants and animals that live there. Why are these plants and animals able to live where they do? **2.a**

**Writing**  ELA–WS 2.1

## Write a Story

1. Write a story about a forest animal.
2. Tell where it lives, what it eats, and what it does.
3. Draw pictures that show the animal in the forest.
4. Share your story with the class.

*This bear lives in the forest with her mom and her brother.*

**123** **Math** MG 1.0

## Measure Rainfall

1. Deserts get less than 25 centimeters of rain each year. Measure that amount. Mark it on paper.
2. How much rain falls each year where you live? Measure and mark that amount on the paper.
3. Compare the two amounts.

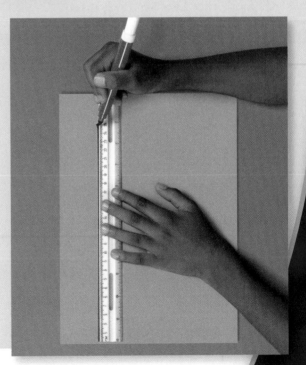

For more links and activities, go to **www.hspscience.com**

# A New Plane Fights Fires

Wildfires burn large parts of forests in the western United States. Wildfires can move quickly. This can put firefighters in danger.

The Altus II is light. It does not need much fuel. It can fly for up to 24 hours at a time.

Find out more. Log on to
**www.hspscience.com**

Now firefighters have a new tool to help them. This tool is a robot plane called Altus II. This plane does not have a pilot. People fly it from the ground.

The Altus II has cameras. It takes pictures of fires. The cameras can see through smoke. They can also see places that might catch fire.

The plane can also be used by people to keep track of floods or hurricanes.

**Think and Write**

How does using Altus II help firefighters?

**SYLVIA EARLE**
▶ California Marine Biologist
▶ Studies ocean plants and animals

# Sylvia Earle

How do you find out what lives in the ocean? You dive in. You observe. You take pictures. This is just what Sylvia Earle and her teams of scientists do. They dive deep into the Pacific Ocean. They study the plants and animals that live there.

Sylvia Earle wants to protect the living things in the ocean. She studies ways oil spills can harm ocean animals. She helps oil companies keep the ocean clean and safe.

## ✍ Think and Write

Why is Sylvia Earle's work important?    2.a

# Ynes Enriquetta Julietta Mexia

Ynes Enriquetta Julietta Mexia was a scientist. She began collecting plants when she was 55 years old. She collected plants from around the world. Many of these plants had never been collected before. Some are named after her.

Ynes Enriquetta Julietta Mexia brought thousands of plants to a college. The plants are in the herbarium there. A herbarium is a place where dried plants are kept. Now other scientists can study the plants.

**YNES ENRIQUETTA JULIETTA MEXIA**

▶ California Botanist
▶ Collected plants

### ✎ Think and Write

How did Ynes Enriquetta Julietta Mexia help other scientists learn about the world's plants? **2.a**

175

# San Diego-La Jolla Underwater Park

San Diego

What kind of park would have no trees or grass? San Diego–La Jolla Underwater Park is a park in the ocean. It was made to protect the things that live underwater. You can swim and use boats in the park, but there is one important rule. Look, but do not touch!

La Jolla Cove is part of the park. The water in the cove is very clean and clear. People work at the park to keep it that way. Thanks to them, you might see a fish swimming 30 feet below your boat!

2.a

# ✏️ Think and Write

What body parts does a fish have that help it live in the ocean?

LA JOLLA
ECOLOGICAL
RESERVE

**SWIMMERS USE CAUTION**
STAY WITHIN BOAT FREE ZONE. FLOATS & SPEARS PROHIBITED IN COVE.

SAN DIEGO-LA JOLLA
UNDERWATER PARK
(ECOLOGICAL RESERVE)

NO PERSON SHALL DISTURB OR TAKE
ANY PLANT, BIRD, MAMMAL, FISH,
MOLLUSK, CRUSTACEAN, OR OTHER
MARINE LIFE.
GEOLOGICAL FORMATIONS AND
ARCHAELOGICAL ARTIFACTS MAY NOT
BE DISTURBED OR MOVED.

SECTION 1583. CALIF. FISH & GAME CODE
SECTION 632. T. 14. CALIF. ADMINISTRATIVE CODE

**LESSON 4**

## Science Content

**2.c** *Students know* animals eat plants or other animals for food and may also use plants or even other animals for shelter and nesting.

## Investigation and Experimentation

**4.b** Record observations and data with pictures, numbers, or written statements.

# How Do Living Things Help Each Other?

## California Fast Fact

### Porcupines

Porcupines have quills on their bodies. They use their quills to keep safe from other animals. The quills also help porcupines float in water.

## Vocabulary Preview

**pollen** p. 184

**food chain** p. 186

porcupine

179

# Animals in a Tree

## Ask a Question

How are these animals using plants?

blue jay

deer

## Get Ready

**Investigation Skill Tip**
When you observe, you use your senses to find out about things. You can use pictures, numbers, or words to record what you see.

### You need

hand lens

heron

## What to Do

**Step ①**

With your class, find a tree. **Observe** it with a hand lens. Record what you see.

**Step ②**

Sit quietly. Observe the animals in the tree. Record what they are doing.

**Step ③**

How did the animals use the tree? Talk about what you observed.

## Draw Conclusions

What did you find out about how animals use trees? 2.c

**Independent Inquiry**

**Observe** ways that people use trees. Use pictures or writing to record what you see. 4.b

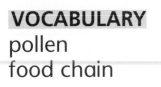
**VOCABULARY**
pollen
food chain

⭐ **MAIN IDEA AND DETAILS**
Look for the main ideas about how living things help each other.

# Living Together

Plants and animals live together in an environment. Some animals use plants for shelter. Beavers use wood from trees to build dams and lodges.

Many birds build nests in shrubs or trees. Nests help keep the young birds safe.

birds in a nest

beaver building a dam

Some animals use other animals to meet their needs. Fleas live on monkeys. They find food there. Some fish live near other animals. They help keep each other safe.

(Focus Skill) **MAIN IDEA AND DETAILS** What are some ways that animals use plants and other animals?

## Insta-Lab

**Shelters from Plants**
Use plant parts and clay to make a model of a bird's nest. How is your model like a real bird's nest?

Monkeys take fleas off each other.

clown fish near sea anemones

# Animals Help Plants

Some animals help plants make new plants. Animals carry pollen from flower to flower. **Pollen** is a powder that flowers need to make seeds.

honey possum carrying pollen

butterfly carrying pollen

Some animals help plants by carrying seeds. Animals take the seeds to new places. There, the seeds may grow into new plants.

**Focus Skill** **MAIN IDEA AND DETAILS** How can animals help plants make new plants?

squirrel carrying seeds

dog carrying seeds

# Food Chains

Animals eat plants or other animals. A **food chain** shows the things animals eat. Look at this food chain. The grass uses sunlight to make its own food. The grasshopper eats the grass. The frog eats the grasshopper. The snake eats the frog. The hawk eats the snake.

**Focus Skill** **MAIN IDEA AND DETAILS** What does a food chain show?

## Essential Question

**How do living things help each other?**

In this lesson, you learned that animals use plants and other animals to meet their needs.

**Science Content Standards in This Lesson**

2.c *Students know* animals eat plants or other animals for food and may also use plants or even other animals for shelter and nesting.

**1.** (Focus Skill) **MAIN IDEA AND DETAILS**

Make a chart like this one. Tell how animals use plants and other animals to meet their needs. 2.c

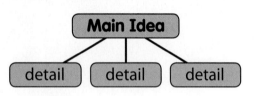

**2. DRAW CONCLUSIONS**

What does every food chain start with? 2.c

**3. VOCABULARY** Use the word **pollen** to tell about this picture. 2.c

**4. Critical Thinking**

Number the picture to show a food chain. 2.c

**5.** How do bees help plants make new plants? 2.c

A by building a dam
B by carrying pollen
C by making a nest
D by using them for shelter

## The Big Idea

**6.** Draw a picture of an animal. Show how it uses a plant or another animal to meet its needs. 2.c

### ✏️ Writing 🐻 ELA–W.S. 2.2

## Write to Inform

1. Think of a way you have used plants or animals today. Draw pictures and write sentences to tell how.

2. Put your pages together to make a book.

3. Share your book with your classmates.

### 123 Math 🐻 NS 2.6, AF 1.0

## Solve a Problem

1. Grizzly bears eat about 24 pounds of plants each day.

2. They also eat 6 pounds of meat each day.

3. How many pounds of food in all does a grizzly bear eat each day?

4. Write a number sentence to show how you solved the problem.

🖱️ For more links and activities, go to **www.hspscience.com**

# Wrap-Up

## ▶ Visual Summary

Tell how each picture helps explain the **Big Idea**.

**The Big Idea** Plants and animals need some things to live and grow. They meet their needs in different ways.

**2.b, 2.e**

Plants need water, light, and air. Roots take in water. Leaves take in light and air. Animals need water, food, air, and shelter.

**2.a**

Plants and animals can live in different kinds of places. They have parts that help them live where they do.

**2.c, 2.d**

Animals eat plants or other animals for food. An animal's teeth show what kind of food it eats. Animals with flat teeth eat plants. Animals with sharp teeth eat meat. Animals also use plants or other animals for shelter.

# Show What You Know

Unit Writing Activity

## Write a Paragraph That Describes Teeth

Look at teeth in library books. Observe models of teeth. Then write a paragraph about all the teeth you observe. Tell how they are alike and how they are different. Tell what you can learn by observing teeth. Draw pictures to go with your paragraph.

Unit Project

## Make a Terrarium

A terrarium is a closed container in which small plants and animals can meet their needs. You can make one with a plastic bottle or a tank. Put in some soil and some plants that grow where you live. Add insects or other animals. Put a lid on the terrarium. Observe it each week. Write about ways the plants help the animals.

# Vocabulary Review

Use the words to complete the sentences. The page numbers tell where to look if you need help.

**roots** p. 140          **shelter** p. 153

**leaves** p. 141          **desert** p. 166

1. The _____ are plant parts that take in water and nutrients.          2.e

2. A _____ is land that gets little rain.          2.a

3. The _____ are plant parts that take in light and air to make food for the plant.          2.e

4. A place where an animal can be safe is a _____.          2.b

# Check Understanding

**5.** What do plants need to make food?　　　2.b

   **A** light, air, water

   **B** light, food, air

   **C** shelter, food, water

   **D** water, light, shelter

**6.** Describe one way that plants and animals help each other.　　2.c

# Critical Thinking

**7.** Look at this horse's teeth. Infer what the horse eats from the shape of its teeth.　　2.d

## The Big Idea

**8.** How do the living things in these places meet their needs?

# Weather

**3** Weather can be observed, measured, and described. As a basis for understanding this concept:

**3.a** *Students know* how to use simple tools (e.g., thermometer, wind vane) to measure weather conditions and record changes from day to day and across the seasons.

**3.b** *Students know* that the weather changes from day to day but that trends in temperature or rain (or snow) tend to be predictable during a season.

**3.c** *Students know* the sun warms the land, air, and water.

This unit also includes these Investigation and Experimentation Standards:

**4.b**, **4.c**, **4.e**

## What's the Big Idea?

People can observe, measure, and describe weather.

## Essential Questions

Dana Point Harbor

Dear Sumi,

My family and I went sailing today. The weather was sunny and warm. There was a nice breeze, too. We had fun!

Your friend,

Ana

Read Ana's postcard. What did Ana learn about weather? How do you think that helps explain the **Big Idea?**

**Unit Inquiry**

## Evaporation
How does the shape of a puddle affect evaporation? Plan and do a test to find out.

LESSON

**1**

## Science Content

**3.b** *Students know* that
the weather changes from
day to day but that trends
in temperature or rain (or
snow) tend to be predictable
during a season.

## Investigation and Experimentation

**4.b** Record observations
and data with pictures,
numbers, or written
statements.

**4.c** Record observations
on a bar graph.

Essential Question

# How Does Weather Change from Day to Day?

## California Fast Fact

**Mojave Desert**
In most years, the
Mojave Desert
gets less than 15
centimeters (6
inches) of rain. Most
of that rain falls in
winter.

Mojave Desert

## Vocabulary Preview

**weather** p. 200

**predict** p. 203

197

# Daily Weather

**Directed Inquiry**

## Ask a Question

What is the weather in the photograph like?

## Get Ready

**Investigation Skill Tip**
When you predict, you use what you know to guess what will happen.

**You need**

paper

markers

## What to Do

**Step ①**

Observe the weather each day for two weeks.

**Step ②**

Make a bar graph. Record what you observed.

**Step ③**

Compare the weather from day to day. Look for patterns on your graph. **Predict** next week's weather. Next week, check to see if your predictions are correct.

## Draw Conclusions

What did you find out about predicting weather? 3.b

**Independent Inquiry**

Observe the weather each day in the morning and in the late afternoon. What can you tell about the weather each day? 4.b

**VOCABULARY**
weather
predict

Focus Skill **COMPARE AND CONTRAST**

Look for ways weather can be different from day to day.

# Weather

**Weather** is what the air outside is like. You can see and feel the weather.

sunny

rainy

Weather may be warm or cool.
It may be sunny or cloudy. Weather
may also be snowy, windy, or rainy.

**Focus Skill** **COMPARE AND CONTRAST** What are some
different kinds of weather?

snowy

windy

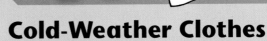

Insta-Lab

**Cold-Weather Clothes**
Draw a picture of
yourself outdoors on a
cold day. Label each thing
you wear to stay warm.
Then show your work to
a partner. How does each
piece of clothing help
keep you warm?

# Weather Changes

What is the weather like today? Is it warm or cool? Is it sunny or cloudy? Is it rainy, windy, or snowy?

Weather can change. It may be sunny one day. The next day may be cloudy. Weather can change in just a few hours or over many months.

A change in weather that keeps repeating is a weather pattern. You can predict the weather with weather patterns. To **predict** is to use what you know to guess what will happen.

**Focus Skill COMPARE AND CONTRAST** How can weather be different from day to day?

## Essential Question

**How does weather change from day to day?**

In this lesson, you learned that weather may be sunny, cloudy, windy, rainy, or snowy. You also learned that weather changes from day to day.

**Science Content Standards in This Lesson**

**3.b** *Students know* that the weather changes from day to day but that trends in temperature or rain (or snow) tend to be predictable during a season.

---

**1.** **Focus Skill** **COMPARE AND CONTRAST** Make a chart like this one. Show how weather can change from day to day. **3.b**

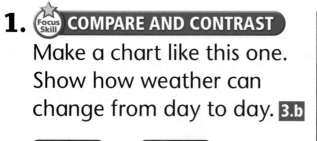

**2.** **SUMMARIZE** Write a summary. Tell what you learned about weather. **3.b**

**3.** **VOCABULARY** Tell about the **weather** in this picture. **3.b**

**4.** **Investigation** How can a bar graph help you record what you observe? **4.c**

**5.** There are no clouds. What is the weather like? **3.b**
  **A** It is cloudy.
  **B** It is rainy.
  **C** It is snowy.
  **D** It is sunny.

## The **Big Idea**

**6.** Draw a picture to show how weather can change from day to day. **3.b**

**Writing** ELA–WS 2.2

### Write to Inform

1. Think about your favorite kind of weather.

2. Write about it. Start each line with a letter of a word for that weather.

3. Tell why you like that kind of weather.

**Math** SDAP 1.0, 1.2

### Graph Activities

1. Make a list of things you like to do in summer.

2. Ask your classmates which of the activities they like the best.

3. Make a tally chart. Show how many people like each activity the best.

4. Use the data to make a bar graph.

For more links and activities, go to **www.hspscience.com**

# California Standards in This Lesson

## Science Content

**3.b** *Students know* that the weather changes from day to day but that trends in temperature or rain (or snow) tend to be predictable during a season.

## Investigation and Experimentation

**4.b** Record observations and data with pictures, numbers, or written statements.

**4.e** Make new observations when discrepancies exist between two descriptions of the same object or phenomenon.

## California Fast Fact

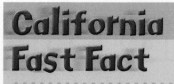

**Mount Shasta**

Mount Shasta has warm, dry summers. It has wet, cold winters. Each year, it may get as much as 244 centimeters (96 inches) of snow.

Essential Question

# How Does Weather Change with Each Season?

Mount Shasta

## Vocabulary Preview

**season** p. 210

207

# How to Stay Warm

## Ask a Question

People dress for the weather. What weather are these people dressed for?

## Get Ready

**Investigation Skill Tip**
To draw a conclusion, use what you observe to decide what something means.

### You need

plastic bag

ice water

mitten

## What to Do

**Step 1**

Put your hand in the bag. Dip the bag into the water. How does your hand feel?

**Step 2**

Put on the mitten. Repeat Step 1. How does your hand feel?

**Step 3**

Compare your answers with a classmate's answers. If you get different answers, repeat the Investigate.

## Draw Conclusions

What is winter weather like? **Draw a conclusion** about what can help keep you warm in winter. **3.b**

**Independent Inquiry**

What do people do in summer? Look at the seasons picture cards. **Infer** which cards show summer. **4.b**

**VOCABULARY**
season

**SEQUENCE**

Look for the order of the seasons and how weather changes from season to season.

# Seasons

A **season** is a time of year. A year has four seasons. The seasons are spring, summer, fall, and winter. They form a pattern. After every winter, spring comes.

**SEQUENCE** What season comes after summer?

Spring starts in the month of March.

# Science Up Close

## Seasons

spring

summer

fall

winter

For more links and animations, go to **www.hspscience.com**

# Spring

The weather changes from season to season. You can predict what the weather will be like in each season. In spring, the air gets warmer. In some places, spring weather is very rainy.

spring

**Focus Skill** **SEQUENCE** How does the air change in spring?

# Summer

Summer comes after spring. Summer is usually the warmest time of the year. Summer days are often hot and sunny. In summer, storms can quickly change the weather.

summer

 **SEQUENCE** Which season comes after spring?

## Insta-Lab

### New Leaves
Observe a plant stem or branch in spring. Use a hand lens and a tape measure. Observe the size, shape, and color of the new leaves. How will the leaves change as they grow?

213

# Fall

Fall is the next season. In fall, the air gets cooler. Some fall days are sunny. Some other fall days are cloudy.

**Focus Skill** **SEQUENCE** How does weather change from summer to fall?

fall

# Winter

Winter comes after fall. Winter is the coldest season.

In some places, snow falls. In other places, the air cools down just a little. It does not snow there.

Spring comes again after winter. The pattern of changes from season to season repeats.

winter

**SEQUENCE** What happens when winter ends?

215

## Essential Question

**How does weather change with each season?**

In this lesson, you learned that the weather for each season can be predicted.

**Science Content Standards in This Lesson**

**3.b** *Students know* that the weather changes from day to day but that trends in temperature or rain (or snow) tend to be predictable during a season.

1. (Focus Skill) **SEQUENCE** Make a chart like this one. Tell how weather changes with the seasons. **3.b**

2. **DRAW CONCLUSIONS** Why can you predict what the weather will be like in each season? **3.b**

3. **VOCABULARY** Use the word **season** to tell about this picture. **3.b**

4. **Investigation** Why is it important to compare your answers with a classmate's answers? **4.e**

5. How is winter different in different places? **3.b**

The **Big Idea**

6. Fold a sheet of paper into four parts. Draw pictures to show the weather for each season. **3.b**

### Writing · ELA–WS 2.2

**Write to Inform**

1. Think about what one season is like where you live. Write a weather report for one day of that season.

2. Present your weather report to the class. Use a map to point out your city.

### Math · NS 1.1

**Use a Calendar**

1. Use a calendar to answer these questions.

2. How many months are there in summer? What are their names?

3. When does summer begin? When does it end?

For more links and activities, go to **www.hspscience.com**

# Weather Satellites

weather satellite

Weather satellites fly very high above Earth. Some weather satellites fly around Earth from the North Pole to the South Pole. Other weather satellites stay above the same place on Earth.

Weather satellites carry cameras that take pictures of Earth. The pictures show clouds in the air. They show snow and ice on the ground. They also show where storms are forming. The satellites send these pictures to Earth. Weather scientists use the pictures to help them predict what the weather will be.

## ✍️ Think and Write

How do weather satellites help scientists predict the weather? **3.a**

picture taken from a weather satellite

# June Bacon-Bercey

**JUNE BACON-BERCEY**

▶ California Meteorologist

▶ Expert on weather and flying

June Bacon-Bercey is a science teacher in California. Many of her students do not know that she is also a famous weather scientist.

June Bacon-Bercey started as a TV weather reporter. Later, she became an expert on weather and flying. She has won awards. She also has started an award of her own. Each year, this award gives money to a woman who wants to become a weather scientist like her.

## ✍ Think and Write

Why is weather important to flying?

# Bob Stokes

Bob Stokes is a special kind of scientist. He studies the weather. He can tell when the weather will change.

**BOB STOKES**
▶ **Meteorologist**
▶ Studies and predicts the weather

Bob Stokes also studies weather patterns so he can predict weather. He can tell when a thunderstorm might happen. Thunderstorms can bring strong wind and heavy rain. They can harm people and their homes. If people know what kind of weather is coming, they can stay safe. Bob Stokes is helping people do that.

## Think and Write

Why is predicting the weather important?    3.b

## Science Content

**3.a** *Students know* how to use simple tools (e.g., thermometer, wind vane) to measure weather conditions and record changes from day to day and across the seasons.

## Investigation and Experimentation

**4.b** Record observations and data with pictures, numbers, or written statements.

**Essential Question**

# How Can We Measure Weather?

## California Fast Fact

### World's Largest Thermometer

The world's largest thermometer is 134 feet (41 meters) tall. It is as many feet tall as the highest U.S. temperature ever recorded.

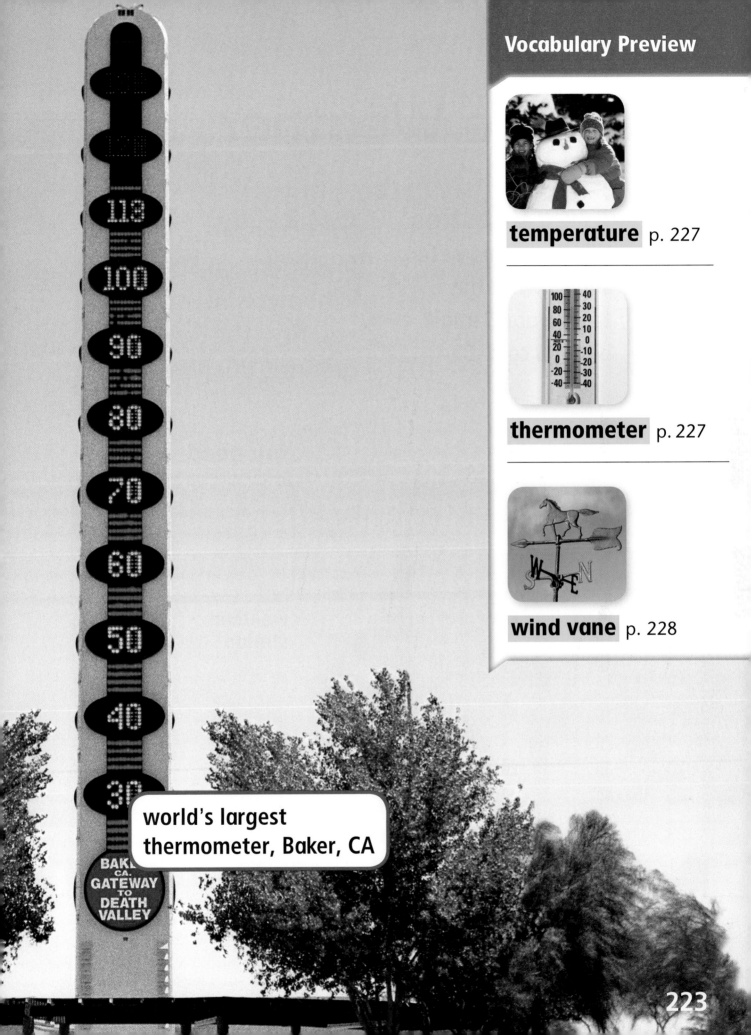

**temperature** p. 227

**thermometer** p. 227

**wind vane** p. 228

world's largest
thermometer, Baker, CA

BAKER
CA.
GATEWAY
TO
DEATH
VALLEY

# Measure Weather

## Ask a Question

Which thermometer shows what the temperature might be on a cold day?

## Get Ready

**Investigation Skill Tip**
When you measure, you find the size or amount of something.

**You need**

weather station

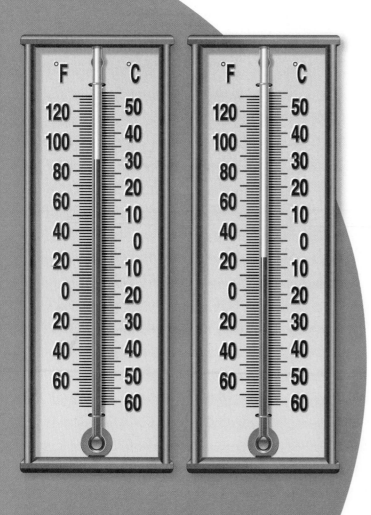

## What to Do

**Step ①**

Measure the weather each day for five days. Use a thermometer, a wind vane, and a rain gauge or a weather station.

**Step ②**

Use numbers and words to record your measurements.

**Step ③**

How did the weather change from day to day? Share your information.

## Draw Conclusions

How do tools help you measure weather?  3.a

**Independent Inquiry**

Measure the weather in different seasons. Record your measurements. How did the weather change with the seasons?  4.b

**VOCABULARY**
temperature
thermometer
wind vane

**Focus Skill MAIN IDEA AND DETAILS**

Look for the main ideas about measuring weather.

# Measuring Weather

You can use tools to measure weather. Measuring weather helps you see patterns. Patterns help you predict the weather.

**Focus Skill MAIN IDEA AND DETAILS** What does measuring weather help you do?

measuring rainfall

# Measuring Temperature

One way to measure weather is to find the temperature. **Temperature** is the measure of how hot or cold something is.

A **thermometer** is a tool for measuring temperature. You look at the numbers to see how hot or cold the air is. Hot air makes the colored liquid go up. Cold air makes the colored liquid go down.

**Focus Skill** **MAIN IDEA AND DETAILS** How can you find out how warm the air outside is?

thermometer

# Measuring Wind

You can measure wind, too. Wind is moving air. A **wind vane** shows which way the wind is blowing from. The wind turns the arrow on the wind vane. The arrow points to the direction the wind is coming from.

(Focus Skill) **MAIN IDEA AND DETAILS** What tool measures the direction of the wind?

wind vane

# Measuring Rain

You can use a rain gauge to measure how much rain falls. A rain gauge catches rain. The numbers show how much rain has fallen.

(Focus Skill) **MAIN IDEA AND DETAILS** What tool can you use to measure how much rain has fallen?

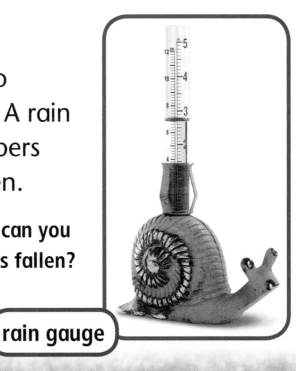

rain gauge

## Insta-Lab

### Make a Rain Gauge

Tape a ruler to the outside of a jar. Put the jar outside before it rains. After it rains, use the ruler to measure how much rain fell. How is this tool like a rain gauge?

**How can we measure weather?**

In this lesson, you learned how to use a thermometer, a wind vane, and a rain gauge to measure weather.

**Science Content Standards in This Lesson**

**3.a** *Students know* how to use simple tools (e.g., thermometer, wind vane) to measure weather conditions and record changes from day to day and across the seasons.

**1.** **Focus Skill MAIN IDEA AND DETAILS**

Make a chart like this one. Show the details of this main idea. **You can use tools to measure weather.** **3.a**

Main Idea
detail    detail    detail

**2.** **SUMMARIZE** Tell some ways you can measure weather. **3.a**

**3.** **VOCABULARY**
Use the words **thermometer** and **temperature** to tell about this picture. **3.a**

**4.** **Critical Thinking** How can measuring weather help people? **3.a**

**5.** Which tool would you use to measure how much rain had fallen? **3.a**

**A** hand lens
**B** rain gauge
**C** thermometer
**D** wind vane

The **Big Idea**

**6.** What are three tools you can use to measure weather? **3.a**

## Write to Describe

1. Find information about temperature, wind, and rainfall in your city last year.

2. Use the data to predict what the weather will be in each month of next year.

3. Write your predictions.

### My Predictions

| Month | Temperature | Wind | Rainfall |
|---|---|---|---|
| January | | | |
| February | | | |
| March | | | |
| April | | | |
| May | | | |
| June | | | |
| July | | | |
| August | | | |
| September | | | |
| October | | | |
| November | | | |
| December | | | |

## Make a Bar Graph

1. This chart shows the amount of rainfall for a city in some months.

2. Use the data to make a bar graph.

3. Share your graph with the class.

### Los Angeles

| month | rainfall in inches |
|---|---|
| January | 3 |
| February | 2 |
| October | 0 |
| November | 1 |

For more links and activities, go to **www.hspscience.com**

# Extreme Weather Differences

Boca

Death Valley

Death Valley

California is a big state. Places in it have different weather. In some places, the temperature gets very high. In other places, it gets very low.

Death Valley is one of the hottest places on Earth. The temperature there can be higher than 100 degrees. One day, it reached 134 degrees! That is the highest temperature ever recorded in the United States.

Boca is in the mountains of the Sierra Nevada. In winter, the temperature there is often below freezing. One time, it was 45 degrees below zero! That is the lowest temperature ever recorded in California.

Boca

✏️ **Think and Write**

Is the weather in your part of California more like Death Valley or Boca? 3.b

LESSON
4

## Science Content

**3.c** *Students know* the sun warms the land, air, and water.

## Investigation and Experimentation

**4.b** Record observations and data with pictures, numbers, or written statements.

Essential Question

# How Does the Sun Cause Weather?

## California Fast Fact

**Donner Lake**

Donner Lake is in Truckee, CA. In the spring, heat from the sun melts the snow at Donner Lake.

**water cycle** p. 242

Donner Lake

# Heat from the Sun

## Ask a Question

What is the sun warming in this picture?

## Get Ready

**Investigation Skill Tip**
When you plan an investigation, you think of what you need to do to find out what you want to know.

**You need**

cup of soil

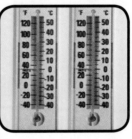

2 thermometers

## What to Do

**Step ❶**

Does the sun warm soil faster than it warms air? **Plan an investigation** to find out. Write the steps of your plan.

**Step ❷**

Follow your plan to try out your ideas.

**Step ❸**

Record what you observe. Share with the class what you learn.

## Draw Conclusions

What did you find out about how the sun warms land and air? **3.c**

**Independent Inquiry**

Put two cups filled with water in a sunny place. Cover one cup. **Observe** the water the next day. **Infer** what happened. **4.b**

**VOCABULARY**
water cycle

**Focus Skill** **CAUSE AND EFFECT**

Look for ways the sun causes weather.

# Heat from the Sun

Most energy on Earth comes from the sun. The sun gives off light and heat.

energy from the sun

Heat makes things warmer. Heat from the sun warms Earth's land, air, and water.

**(Focus Skill) CAUSE AND EFFECT** What does the sun warm?

**Insta-Lab**

**Where's the Heat?**
Use a thermometer. Measure the temperature in different places in your classroom. Find the warmest place. What did you find out?

# The Sun Causes Weather

The sun causes changes in temperature. The sun warms the land. Then the air above the land gets warmer.

On a sunny day, this street gets hot.

On a cloudy day, this street may stay cool all day.

Warming the air causes wind. The wind moves the clouds. Some of the clouds bring rain.

**Focus Skill** **CAUSE AND EFFECT** How does the sun cause weather?

# The Water Cycle

Clouds and rain are part of the water cycle. In the **water cycle**, water moves from Earth to the air and back again.

**Focus Skill** **CAUSE AND EFFECT** What causes water to evaporate?

## Science Up Close

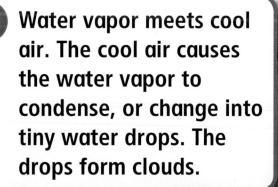

**2** Water vapor meets cool air. The cool air causes the water vapor to condense, or change into tiny water drops. The drops form clouds.

**1** The sun makes water warm. This causes the water to evaporate, or change to water vapor. Water vapor is water in the air that you can not see.

For more links and animations, go to www.hspscience.com

**3** Water drops come together and get bigger and heavier. Then they fall as rain or snow.

**4** Some rain and snow falls into rivers, lakes, and oceans. Some falls on land and then flows into rivers, lakes, and oceans.

**5** The water cycle begins again.

## Essential Question

**How does the sun cause weather?**

In this lesson, you learned that the sun warms the land, air, and water. You also learned how the sun causes weather.

**Science Content Standards in This Lesson**

3.c *Students know* the sun warms the land, air, and water.

**1.** (Focus Skill) **CAUSE AND EFFECT** Make a chart like this one. When the sun shines on Earth, what are the effects? 3.c

cause ⟶ effect

**2. DRAW CONCLUSIONS** What happens to water after it falls to Earth? 3.c

**A** It turns into rain.
**B** It turns into snow.
**C** The sun makes the water warm.
**D** Water drops come together.

**3. VOCABULARY** Explain what happens in the **water cycle**. 3.c

**4. Critical Thinking** What would Earth be like if there were no sun? 3.c

**5.** How does water move from the land to the air and back again? 3.c

**A** in the clouds
**B** in the ocean
**C** in the rain
**D** in the water cycle

## The Big Idea

**6.** How does the sun cause weather? 3.c

**Writing**     ELA–WS 2.2

## Write to Inform

1. Read about the sun. Then write a short report about what you learned.

2. Tell what the sun is and where it is. Also, tell what the sun does.

3. Draw pictures to go with your report.

The sun is a star.

**1₂3 Math**     AF 1.0, 1.1

## Solve Problems

1. Juan checked his rain gauge. He saw that 5 centimeters of rain fell on Monday and 3 centimeters fell on Tuesday.

2. How much rain fell in all?

3. Write a number sentence to help you solve the problem.

For more links and activities, go to **www.hspscience.com**

# Wrap-Up

## ▶Visual Summary

Tell how each picture helps explain the **Big Idea**.

**The Big Idea** People can observe, measure, and describe weather.

**3.a**

You can use tools to observe and record things about the weather. A thermometer measures temperature.

**3.c**

The sun warms land, air, and water. Heat from the sun causes weather. It causes changes in temperature.

**3.b**

Weather changes from day to day. Weather also changes from season to season. You can predict what the weather will be like in each season. The weather in each season is the same year after year.

# Show What You Know

✎ **Unit Writing Activity**

## Write a Story About a Raindrop

Think about a raindrop. What does its cloud look like? Where does the raindrop land when it falls to Earth? Where does it go on Earth? Draw pictures. Show the raindrop in each part of the water cycle.

## Unit Project

### Record Data for a Week of Weather

Make a weather chart for one week. Check the temperature and the wind. Is it cloudy or sunny? Is it raining or snowing? Give a weather report to the class. Repeat in three months. Then compare your two charts. Predict what the weather will be like in another three months.

| Monday | 82 degrees sunny calm | |
| Tuesday | 79 degrees cloudy light breeze | |
| Wednesday | 78 degrees cloudy 4 centimeters of rain strong breeze | |
| Thursday | 80 degrees cloudy light breeze | |
| Friday | 81 degrees sunny light breeze | |

## Vocabulary Review

Use the words to complete the sentences. The page numbers tell you where to look if you need help.

**weather** p. 200    **temperature** p. 227

**predict** p. 203    **thermometer** p. 227

**season** p. 210    **water cycle** p. 242

**1.** A _____ is a tool for measuring temperature.    **3.a**

**2.** A _____ is a time of year.    **3.b**

**3.** The _____ is what the air outside is like.    **3.b**

**4.** The _____ is the way water moves from Earth to the air and then back again.    **3.c**

**5.** You _____ when you use what you know to guess what will happen.    **3.b**

**6.** The _____ of something is the measure of how hot or cold it is.    **3.a**

## Check Understanding

**7.** How does weather change between summer and fall?　3.b

   **A** It gets cold enough to snow in fall.

   **B** It gets cooler in the fall.

   **C** It gets warmer in the fall.

   **D** The weather is the same in both seasons.

**8.** Tell what each of these tools is used for.　   3.a

## Critical Thinking

**9.** In what ways can weather change from day to day?　3.b

## The Big Idea

**10.** Tell how the sun causes weather.

# References

## Contents

### Health Handbook

### Reading in Science Handbook

### Math in Science Handbook ... R20

# Your Senses

You have five senses that tell you about the world. Your five senses are sight, hearing, smell, taste, and touch.

## Your Eyes

If you look at your eyes in a mirror, you will see an outer white part, a colored part called the iris, and a dark hole in the middle. This hole is called the pupil.

### Caring for Your Eyes

- Have a doctor check your eyes to find out if they are healthy.

- Never look directly at the sun or at very bright lights.

- Wear sunglasses outdoors in bright sunlight and on snow and water.

- Don't touch or rub your eyes.

- Protect your eyes when you play sports.

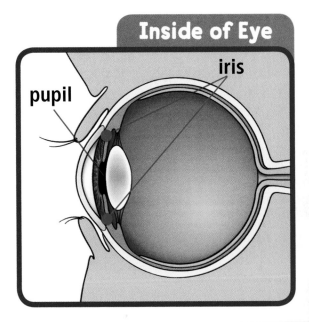

**Inside of Eye**

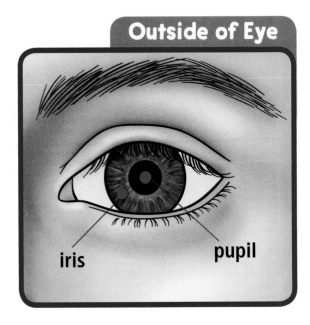

**Outside of Eye**

# Your Senses

## Your Ears

Your ears let you hear the things around you. You can see only a small part of the ear on the outside of your head. The parts of your ear inside your head are the parts that let you hear.

## Caring for Your Ears

• Have a doctor check your ears.

• Avoid very loud noises.

• Never put anything in your ears.

• Protect your ears when you play sports.

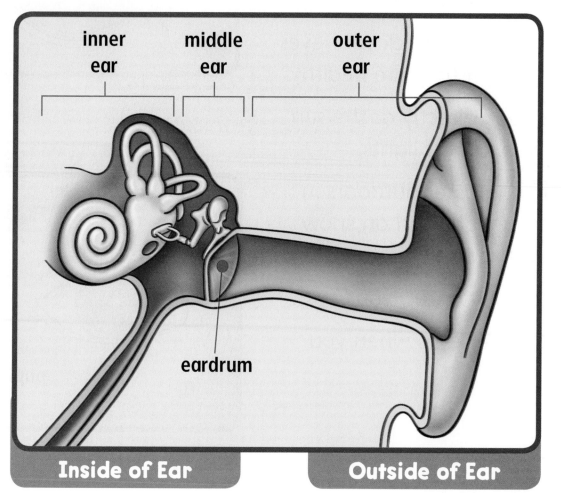

inner ear     middle ear     outer ear

eardrum

**Inside of Ear**      **Outside of Ear**

## Your Senses of Smell and Taste

Your nose cleans the air you breathe and lets you smell things. Your nose and tongue help you taste things you eat and drink.

## Your Skin

Your skin protects your body from germs. Your skin also gives you your sense of touch.

### Caring for Your Skin

- Always wash your hands after coughing or blowing your nose, touching an animal, playing outside, or using the restroom.

- Protect your skin from sunburn. Wear a hat and clothes to cover your skin outdoors.

- Use sunscreen to protect your skin from the sun.

- Wear proper safety pads and a helmet when you play sports, ride a bike, or skate.

# Your Skeletal System

Inside your body are many hard, strong bones. They form your skeletal system. The bones in your body protect parts inside your body.

Your skeletal system works with your muscular system to hold your body up and to give it shape.

## Caring for Your Skeletal System

- Always wear a helmet and other safety gear when you skate, ride a bike or a scooter, or play sports.

- Eat foods that help keep your bones strong and hard.

- Exercise to help your bones stay strong and healthy.

- Get plenty of rest to help your bones grow.

skull

spine

skull

arm bones

spine (backbone)

hip bones

leg bones

# Your Muscular System

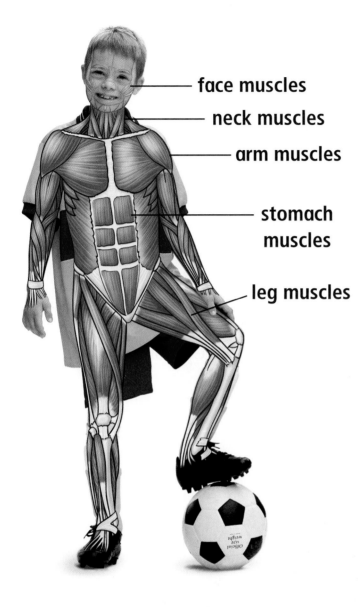

— face muscles

— neck muscles

— arm muscles

— stomach muscles

— leg muscles

Your muscular system is made up of the muscles in your body. Muscles are body parts that help you move.

## Caring for Your Muscular System

- Exercise to keep your muscles strong.

- Eat foods that will help your muscles grow.

- Drink plenty of water when you play sports or exercise.

- Rest your muscles after you exercise or play sports.

# Your Nervous System

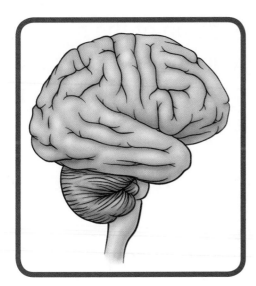

Your brain and your nerves are parts of your nervous system. Your brain keeps your body working. It tells you about the world around you. Your brain also lets you think, remember, and have feelings.

## Caring for Your Nervous System

- Get plenty of sleep. Sleeping lets your brain rest.

- Always wear a helmet to protect your head and your brain when you ride a bike or play sports.

# Your Digestive System

Your digestive system helps your body get energy from the foods you eat. Your body needs energy to do things.

When your body digests food, it breaks the food down. Your digestive system keeps the things your body needs. It also gets rid of the things your body does not need to keep.

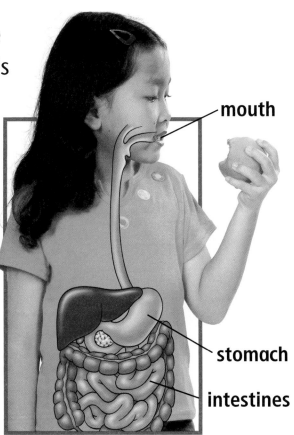

mouth

stomach

intestines

## Caring for Your Digestive System

• Brush and floss your teeth every day.

• Wash your hands before you eat.

• Eat slowly and chew your food well before you swallow.

• Eat vegetables and fruits. They help move foods through your digestive system.

# Your Respiratory System

You breathe using your respiratory system. Your mouth, nose, and lungs are all parts of your respiratory system.

## Caring for Your Respiratory System

- Never put anything in your nose.

- Never smoke.

- Exercise enough to make you breathe harder. Breathing harder makes your lungs stronger.

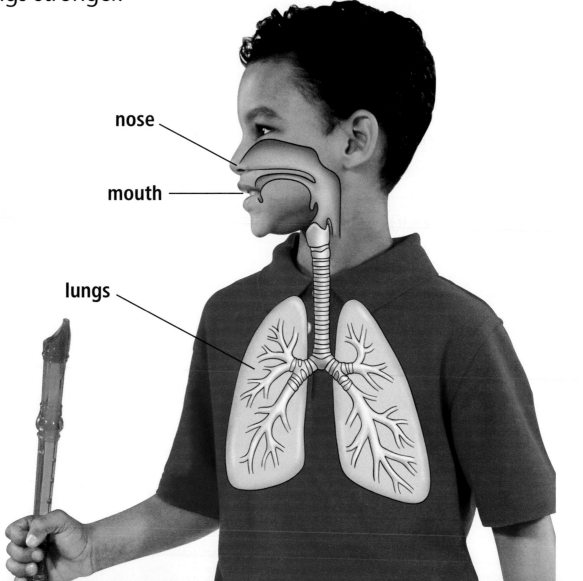

nose

mouth

lungs

# Your Circulatory System

Your circulatory system is made up of your heart and your blood vessels. Your blood carries food energy and oxygen to help your body work. Blood vessels are small tubes. They carry blood from your heart to every part of your body.

Your heart is a muscle. It is beating all the time. As your heart beats, it pumps blood through your blood vessels.

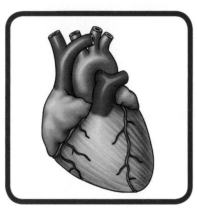

## Caring for Your Circulatory System

• Exercise every day to keep your heart strong.

• Eat meats and green leafy vegetables. They help your blood carry oxygen.

• Never touch anyone else's blood.

# Staying Healthy

You can do many things to help yourself stay fit and healthy.

You can also avoid doing things that can harm you.

If you know ways to stay safe and healthy and you do these things, you can help yourself have good health.

Getting enough rest

Staying away from alcohol, tobacco, and other drugs

Staying active

Keeping clean

Eating right

# Keeping Clean

Keeping clean helps you stay healthy. You can pick up germs from the things you touch. Washing with soap and water helps remove germs from your skin.

Wash your hands for as long as it takes to say your ABCs. Always wash your hands at these times.

• Before and after you eat

• After coughing or blowing your nose

• After using the restroom

• After touching an animal

• After playing outside

# Caring for Your Teeth

Brushing your teeth and gums keeps them clean and healthy. You should brush your teeth at least twice a day. Brush in the morning. Brush before you go to bed at night. It is also good to brush your teeth after you eat if you can.

## Brushing Your Teeth

Use a soft toothbrush that is the right size for you. Always use your own toothbrush. Use only a small amount of toothpaste. It should be about the size of a pea. Be sure to rinse your mouth with water after you brush your teeth.

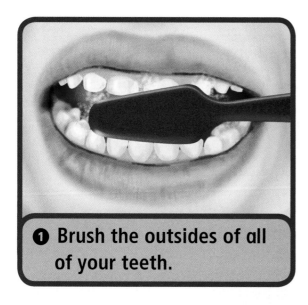

❶ Brush the outsides of all of your teeth.

❷ Brush the insides of all of your teeth.

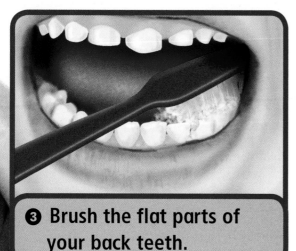

❸ Brush the flat parts of your back teeth.

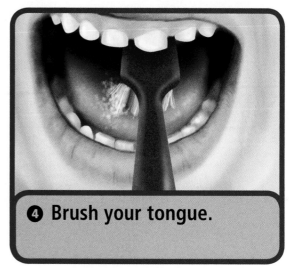

❹ Brush your tongue.

# Identify the Main Idea and Details

Some lessons in this science book are written to help you find the main idea. Learning how to find the main idea can help you understand what you read. The main idea of a paragraph is what it is mostly about. The details tell you more about it.

Read this paragraph.

> Lions are hunters. They hunt for meat to eat. Lions can run very fast. They see and hear very well. They need sharp teeth to catch animals. They have sharp teeth to eat the meat they catch.

This chart shows the main idea and details.

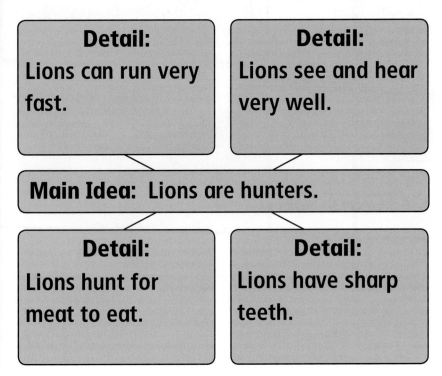

**Detail:** Lions can run very fast.

**Detail:** Lions see and hear very well.

**Main Idea:** Lions are hunters.

**Detail:** Lions hunt for meat to eat.

**Detail:** Lions have sharp teeth.

# Compare and Contrast

Some science lessons are written to help you see how things are alike and different. Learning how to compare and contrast can help you understand what you read.

Read this paragraph.

> Birds and mammals are kinds of animals. Birds have a body covering of feathers. Mammals have a body covering of fur. Both birds and mammals need food, air, and water to live. Most birds can fly. Most mammals walk or run.

Here is how you can compare and contrast birds and mammals.

| **Ways They Are Alike** | **Ways They Are Different** |
| --- | --- |
| **Compare** | **Contrast** |
| Both are kinds of animals. Both need food, air, and water to live. | Birds have feathers. Mammals have fur. Most birds fly. Most mammals walk or run. |

Some science lessons are written to help you understand why things happen. You can use a chart like this to help you find cause and effect.

| **Cause** | **Effect** |
|---|---|
| A cause is why something happens. | An effect is what happens. |

Some paragraphs have more than one cause or effect. Read this paragraph.

> Water can be a solid, a liquid, or a gas. When water is very cold, it turns into solid ice. When water is heated, it turns into water vapor, a gas.

This chart shows two causes and their effects in the paragraph.

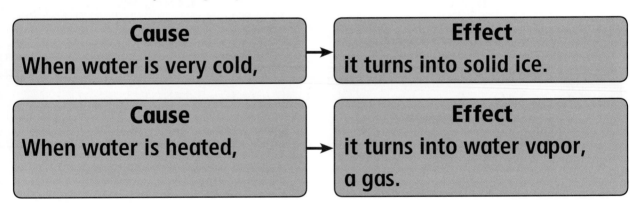

| **Cause** | **Effect** |
|---|---|
| When water is very cold, | it turns into solid ice. |

| **Cause** | **Effect** |
|---|---|
| When water is heated, | it turns into water vapor, a gas. |

 **Sequence**

Learning how to find sequence can help you understand what you read. You can use a chart like this to help you find sequence.

| **1. The first step** | → | **2. The next step** | → | **3. The last step** |

Some paragraphs use words that help you understand order. Read this paragraph. Look at the underlined words.

Each day <u>begins</u> when the sun appears. <u>Then</u> the sun slowly climbs into the sky. At midday, the sun is straight overhead. <u>Then</u> the sun slowly falls back to the horizon. At <u>last</u>, the sun is gone. It is nighttime.

This chart shows the sequence of the paragraph.

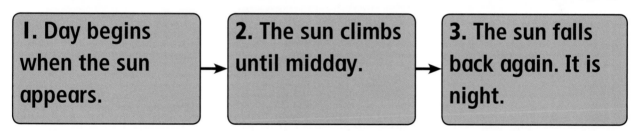

| **1. Day begins when the sun appears.** | → | **2. The sun climbs until midday.** | → | **3. The sun falls back again. It is night.** |

# Draw Conclusions

At the end of some lessons, you will be asked to draw conclusions. When you draw conclusions, you figure something out. To do this, you use what you have learned and your own ideas.

Read this paragraph.

> Birds use their bills to help them get food. Each kind of bird has its own kind of bill. Birds that eat seeds have strong, short bills. Birds that eat bugs have long, sharp bills. Birds that eat water plants have wide, flat bills.

This chart shows how you can draw conclusions.

| **What I Read** | | **What I Know** | | **Conclusion:** |
|---|---|---|---|---|
| Birds use their bills to get food. The bills have different shapes. | + | I have seen ducks up close. They have wide, flat bills. | = | Ducks are birds that eat water plants. |

# Summarize

At the end of some lessons, you will be asked to summarize what you read. In a summary, some sentences tell the main idea. Some sentences tell details.

Read this paragraph.

Honey is made by bees. They gather nectar from flowers. Then they fly home to their beehive with the nectar inside special honey stomachs. The bees put the nectar into special honeycomb holes. Then the bees wait. Soon the nectar will change into sweet, sticky honey. The bees cover the holes with wax that they make. They eat some of the honey during the cold winter.

This chart shows how to summarize what the paragraph is about.

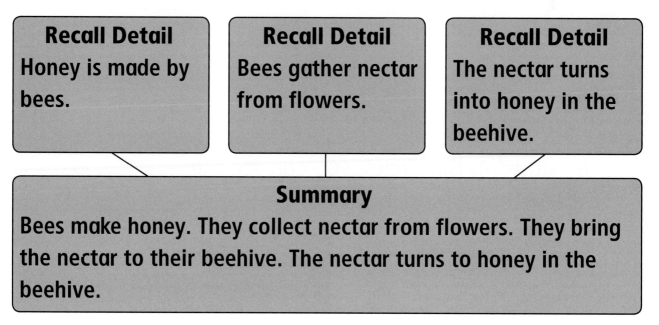

**Recall Detail**
Honey is made by bees.

**Recall Detail**
Bees gather nectar from flowers.

**Recall Detail**
The nectar turns into honey in the beehive.

**Summary**
Bees make honey. They collect nectar from flowers. They bring the nectar to their beehive. The nectar turns to honey in the beehive.

# Using Tables, Charts, and Graphs

## Gather Data

When you investigate in science, you need to collect data.

Suppose you want to find out what kinds of things are in soil. You can sort the things you find into groups.

### Things I Found in One Cup of Soil

Parts of Plants

Small Rocks

Parts of Animals

By studying the circles, you can see the different items found in soil. However, you might display the data in a different way. For example, you could use a tally table.

# Reading a Tally Table

You can show your data in a tally table.

Things I Found in ———— Title
One Cup of Soil

| Items Found | Tally |
|---|---|
| Parts of Plants | JHT I |
| Parts of Animals | III |
| Small Rocks | JHT II |

Tally marks

Data

## How to Read a Tally Table

1. **Read** the tally table. Use the labels.

2. **Study** the data.

3. **Count** the tally marks.

4. **Draw conclusions**. Ask yourself questions like the ones on this page.

## Skills Practice

1. How many parts of plants were found in the soil?

2. How many more small rocks were found in the soil than parts of animals?

3. How many parts of plants and parts of animals were found?

# Using Tables, Charts, and Graphs

## Reading a Bar Graph

People keep many kinds of animals as pets. This bar graph shows the animal groups pets belong to. A bar graph can be used to compare data.

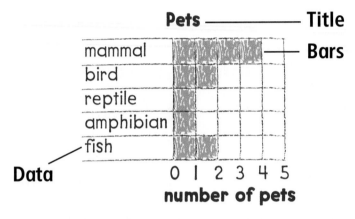

Pets ———— Title

Bars

Data

mammal
bird
reptile
amphibian
fish

0 1 2 3 4 5
**number of pets**

## How to Read a Bar Graph

1. **Look** at the title to learn what kind of information is shown.

2. **Read** the graph. Use the labels.

3. **Study** the data. Compare the bars.

4. **Draw conclusions**. Ask yourself questions like the ones on this page.

## Skills Practice

1. How many pets are mammals?

2. How many pets are birds?

3. How many more pets are mammals than fish?

# Reading a Picture Graph

A second-grade class was asked to choose their favorite season. A picture graph was made to show the results. A picture graph uses pictures to show information.

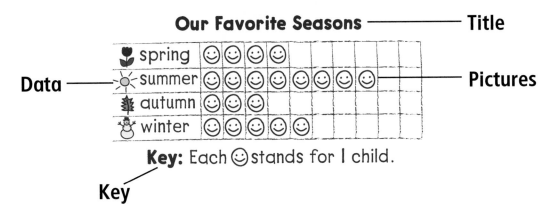

## How to Read a Picture Graph

1. **Look** at the title to learn what kind of information is shown.

2. **Read** the graph. Use the labels.

3. **Study** the data. Compare the number of pictures in each row.

4. **Draw conclusions**. Ask yourself questions like the ones on this page.

## Skills Practice

1. Which season did the most classmates choose?

2. Which season did the fewest classmates choose?

3. How many classmates in all chose summer or winter?

# Measurements

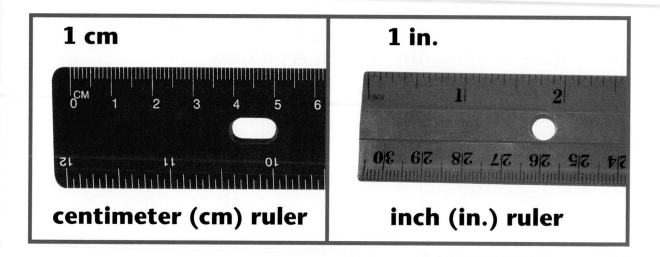

**1 cm**

centimeter (cm) ruler

**1 in.**

inch (in.) ruler

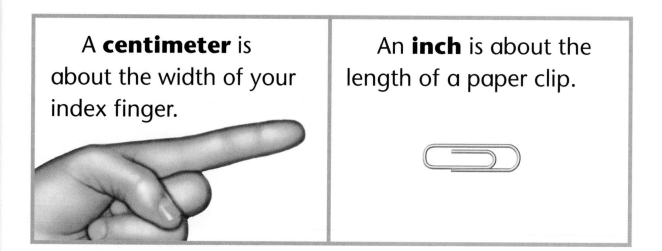

A **centimeter** is about the width of your index finger.

An **inch** is about the length of a paper clip.

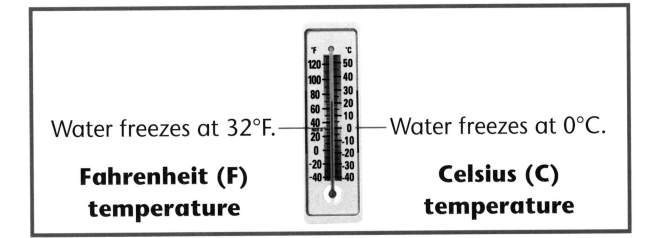

Water freezes at 32°F.

**Fahrenheit (F) temperature**

Water freezes at 0°C.

**Celsius (C) temperature**

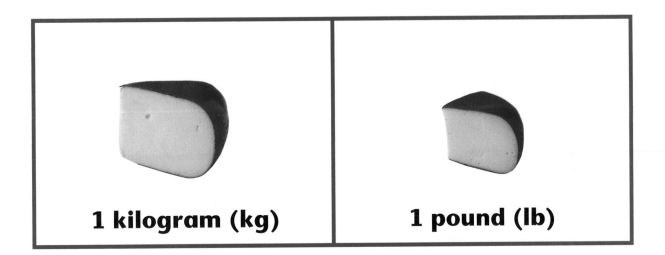

**1 kilogram (kg)**

**1 pound (lb)**

**1 liter (L)**

**1 cup (c)**

# Safety in Science

Here are some safety rules to follow when you do activities.

1. **Think ahead.** Study the steps and follow them.

2. **Be neat and clean.** Wipe up spills right away.

3. **Watch your eyes.** Wear safety goggles when told to do so.

4. **Be careful with sharp things.**

5. **Do not eat or drink things.**

Visit the Multimedia Science Glossary to see illustrations of these words and to hear them pronounced.
**www.hspscience.com**

A glossary lists words in alphabetical order. To find a word, look it up by its first letter or letters.

## A

### above

At a higher place. (30)

### air

A mixture of gases around Earth. (89)

### animal

A living thing that does not make its own food. (148)

## B

### balance

A tool you use to measure the mass of an object. (21)

## bar graph

A graph that helps you compare numbers of things. (43)

## below

At a lower place. (31)

## burn

To change matter into ashes and smoke. (117)

## C

## carnivore

An animal that eats only other animals.

## classify

To group things by how they are alike and different. (6)

## communicate

To draw, speak, or write to tell what you observe. (6)

## compare

To look at things to see how they are alike and different. (9)

## cool

To take away heat. (102)

**D**

## desert

Land that gets very little rain. (166)

## dissolve

To mix completely with a liquid.

## draw conclusions

To use what you observe to figure out what happened. (7)

## dropper

A tool you use to place drops of a liquid. (19)

## E

### environment

All the things that are in a place. (160)

### evaporate

To change from a liquid into a gas. (106 and 242)

## F

### float

To stay on top of a liquid. (78)

### food

Something a living thing needs to live and grow. (136)

### food chain

Shows the food living things eat. (186)

### forceps

A tool you use to separate things. (19)

## forest

Land that is covered with trees. (164)

## freeze

To change from a liquid to a solid. (102)

 **G**

## gas

Matter that will completely fill its container. (88)

**H**

## hand lens

A tool you use to make small objects look bigger. (18)

## heat

Energy that warms. (104)

## herbivore

An animal that eats only plants.

## hypothesize

To tell what you think before you test something. (7)

## infer

To use what you observe to tell why something happened. (11)

## investigation skills

The skills people use to find out things. (6)

# L

## land

The solid part of Earth's surface. (239)

## leaves

The parts of a plant that take in light and air to make food. (141)

## liquid

Matter that takes the shape of its container. (77)

## M

### magnifying box

A tool that makes things you put into it look bigger. (18)

### make a model

To make an object to show how something works. (8)

### mass

The measure of how much matter something has. (58)

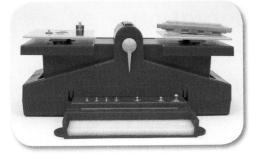

### matter

What everything is made of. (56)

### measure

To find the size or amount of something. (9)

### measuring cup

A tool you use to measure liquid. (20)

## melt

To change from a solid to a liquid. (104)

## mix

To put together. (100)

## mixture

Something that is made up of two or more things. (100)

## nest

(noun) A shelter that birds and some other animals make. (182)

## nest

(verb) To make a home in a shelter. (182)

## observation

Something you learn by using your senses. (10)

## observe

To use your senses to find out about things. (10)

## ocean

A large body of salt water. (168)

**P**

## plan an investigation

To think of a way to check out an idea. (11)

## plant

A living thing that makes its own food. (136)

## pollen

A powder that flowers need to make seeds. (184)

## predator

An animal that hunts other animals for food.

## predict

To use what you know to make a guess about what will happen. (10 and 203)

## property

One part of what something is like. (58)

## roots

The parts of a plant that hold it in the soil and take in water and nutrients. (140)

## ruler

A tool to measure how long or tall an object is. (21)

# R

## rain

Drops of fresh water that fall from clouds. (241)

# S

## science tools

Tools that scientists use to find out things. (18)

## season

A time of year. (210)

## sequence

To put things in the order in which they happen. (8)

## shelter

A place where a person or an animal can be safe. (153)

## sink

To fall to the bottom of a liquid. (79)

## snow

Frozen water that falls from clouds. (243)

## soil

The top layer of Earth. (138)

## solid

A kind of matter that keeps its shape. (67)

## state

A form of matter—solid, liquid, or gas. (50)

## sunlight

Light that comes from the sun. (137)

## tape measure

A tool you use to measure around an object. (21)

## teeth

Parts of the body you use to bite and chew food. (150)

## tell

To share what you observe. (6)

## temperature

The measure of how hot or cold something is. (227)

## thermometer

A tool you use to measure temperature. (20 and 227)

**W**

## water

A clear liquid found in Earth's lakes, rivers, and oceans. (239)

## water cycle

The movement of water from Earth to the air and back again. (242)

## weather

What the air outside is like. (200)

## wind vane

A tool you use to measure the direction of the wind. (228)

# Index

**BEHAVIOR** Sea otters often float together in groups called rafts.

**HABITAT** A sea otter can spend all of its life in the ocean.

**MOVEMENT** A sea otter can dive up to 180 feet (55 meters).

**BEHAVIOR** Sea otters eat clams, crabs, and other ocean animals.